WITH THE WIND
TO THE WEST

The balloon, the size of an eight-storey house, held 5,200 yards of air and was twenty-one yards wide. It was made of 1,500 square yards of fabric, obtained in dozens of department and fabric stores throughout East Germany.

WITH THE WIND TO THE WEST

The Great Balloon Escape

JÜRGEN PETSCHULL

Translated by Courtney Searls

HODDER AND STOUGHTON
LONDON SYDNEY AUCKLAND TORONTO

British Library Cataloguing in Publication Data
Petschull, Jürgen

ISBN 0 340 25895 0

Do you wish to roam farther and farther?
See! The Good lies so near.
Only learn to seize good fortune,
For good fortune's always here.

—Johann Wolfgang von Goethe, *Memoirs*

Contents

WITH THE WIND
TO THE WEST

Introduction

It was without a doubt the most daring escape in the history of divided Germany. Crammed together in a tiny gondola hanging from a colossal homemade balloon, two families crossed the unique boundary that separates Germany from Germany, Communism from Capitalism, and the power blocs of East and West.

"Eight East Germans escape in a hot-air balloon," reported the West German Press Agency in a special announcement on Sunday, September 16, 1979. News of the epic escape circulated quickly, evoking comment throughout the Western world—from the Americas to Australia, from Finland to South Africa. From the East came only awkward silence.

In the West there was an element of vindictive self-satisfaction because the balloon flight took place just before the German Democratic Republic (East Germany) was to celebrate its thirtieth anniversary as a sovereign state—a celebration that promised to be the "most spectacular display of Socialism ever seen on German soil". This coincidence helped make the symbolic flight of the Strelzyk and Wetzel families from Thuringia an international affair.

The New York Times commented that "the escape of the two East German families in a balloon says volumes about the political, economic, and social conditions in the German Democratic Republic".

The *Süddeutsche Zeitung,* one of West Germany's leading newspapers, evaluated the news as "an unprecedented feat, lending bitter commentary to conditions in the very heart of Europe while simultaneously singing a hymn to freedom".

Der Spiegel, a West German magazine that tends toward irony in even the most serious matters, was unusually enthusiastic in its praise: "The sheer, premeditated courage of these two families renders the balloon flight far more spectacular than anything our highly paid stunt men, athletes, or daredevils can offer."

The airborne defectors, however, disagreed with the press. Balloonist Peter Strelzyk, former member of the German Socialist Unity Party and Recognized Activist in Socialist Emulation, did not regard the flight as an act of heroism: "There's nothing heroic about wanting to be free; in any case, our desire for freedom far outweighed our fear."

This book is the result of lengthy interviews with the refugees and extensive research in East and West Germany. It describes the dramatic escape and the events leading up to it, but although it offers a glimpse of everyday life in East Germany, it is not unbiased. The conditions there are described through the subjective eyes of people who felt that they had good reason to flee the hermetically sealed Workers' and Farmers' Republic. These two families felt imprisoned and oppressed in the East, and left—hoping to find freedom in the West.

There are many more in East Germany who empathize with the Strelzyks and Wetzels—many who would cross the border if they could, if there were no wall, no mines, no barbed wire or trip wires.

But there are also some who would not. "Sometimes we forget," writes journalist Eva Windmöller, *Stern* magazine correspondent in East Germany for two years, "that the majority of the seventeen million people living in East Germany have come to terms with the regimented political and social system governing them. Most of them have accepted the German Democratic Republic as their home—just as it is, in spite of its imperfections."

1

With
the Wind
to the West

Early in the morning the humidity was so oppressive that
East Germans sensitive to the weather complained of head-
aches. A cold front streamed in from the north in the late
afternoon, pushing the warm air mass to the mountains in
the Thuringian Forest. By early evening, a violent thunderstorm had struck and the torrential downpour flattened the
unharvested wheat in the fields. A flash of lightning sliced
through a German oak, three feet in diameter, near the
western edge of Pössneck—not far from the mined area on
the frontier between East and West Germany. Then the
storm moved on to the high spruce forests.

The squall was gone as quickly as it had come. Thunder
and lightning disappeared over the mountains, leaving behind a clear and almost cloudless sky. An hour before midnight, stars twinkled and a thin sliver of moon shone above
the little Thuringian town of Pössneck.

Two men in a house on Tuchmacher Street had intently
observed developments in the weather that day, September
15, 1979, and anxiously followed weather predictions on
radio and television. Late at night the Potsdam Central
Weather Service announced the forecast for the German
Democratic Republic: Cold polar air masses caused by a

Scandinavian low pressure area would continue to influence the area. Clear skies and night temperatures as low as thirty-seven degrees Fahrenheit were expected. At ground level, light frost and temperatures plummeting to twenty-eight degrees Fahrenheit were anticipated. One of the men listening to the radio said, "That sounds great! I think tonight may be the right time to finally get the show on the road." His companion, not quite as enthusiastic, answered, "It looks promising, but let's check the wind once more to be sure."

Before leaving the house, the two men donned sweaters and sturdy shoes. One was wearing a brown imitation-leather jacket over his sweater, the other a grey wind-cheater. They drove away in a blue Wartburg with a white roof, East German licence number NK 9743. The East German car passed through quiet streets and left Pössneck travelling south on a narrow country road. A steady wind had already swept the road dry. Once beyond the towns of Wernburg and Ludwigshof, the car turned onto a bumpy stone road. The Wartburg crawled up the incline of the Bahrener Heights in second gear. Just before reaching the barren, 1,800-foot mountaintop, the driver extinguished the headlights and parked the car, and the two men scaled the last few feet on foot—fighting a strong but not too stormy wind.

The two observed the land below them, which was bathed in soft starlight. To the northwest, they could see the reflection of the lights of Weimar, the birthplace of the first German republic in 1919, about nineteen miles away as the crow flies. Directly north, about thirteen miles away, lay the famous university and industrial centre of Jena. To the northeast of Jena, the city of Gera was visible. To the south, they were able to make out only little dots of lights; otherwise, they could see nothing in this direction but the silhouette of the dark landscape against the starlit sky: blunt mountain peaks, woods, and fields—the southern border of the German Democratic Republic.

The man in the imitation-leather jacket licked his right index finger and held it tentatively in the air, while the other in the windcheater tossed a few light-coloured pieces of wool into the air. With the beam of a flashlight, both watched the direction in which the wind carried the pieces of string. They shone the flashlight on a primitive compass and determined that the wind was moving from north-northeast to south-southwest—exactly in the direction of the Federal Republic of Germany (West Germany). They estimated the wind velocity to be between eighteen and twenty-five miles per hour. Pleased with the results of the test, the man in the brown jacket remarked that it would take "about twenty or thirty minutes in the air to get to the other side".

It was almost midnight. Another nondescript Saturday was coming to an end in East and West Germany. Nothing unusual had happened on either side of the border.

News of the day from the Federal Republic of Germany was fairly typical: in the National League playoffs, the champion Hamburg team beats Kaiserslautern one to nothing. Minister of Economics, Count Lambsdorff, "sees no threat to the economic development of West Germany". Cardinal Josef Höffner, Chairman of the German Council of Bishops, again emphasizes that "legalized abortion is licence to murder." The front page of the *Bild* newspaper consisted of an account of a burglary in movie star Claudia Cardinale's Rome mansion, and a story about Hardy Krüger's getting drunk in a Munich nightclub and "dancing across the brightly lit dance floor carrying a silver tray laden with drinks".

News of the day from the German Democratic Republic was no less ordinary: page one of *Neues Deutschland*, the Journal of the Central Committee of the Socialist Unity Party (SED), announced: "Leonid Brezhnev will visit the German Democratic Republic on its thirtieth anniversary. Erich Honecker, Chairman of East Germany's Council of State, sends greetings to comrades in celebration of the day set aside to honour collective farmworkers." On page two was a short article stating that East German citizen Bernhard Twiehoff had been picked up on charges of a border violation and was being held by the authorities for further questioning. Chairman Honecker and Chairman of the East German Cabinet, Willi Stoph, sent congratulations to Sir

Tore Lokoloko, Governor of Papua-New Guinea, on his country's national holiday. In East Germany's major league soccer playoffs, Carl Zeiss-Jena beat First Magdeburg three to two.

It was already past midnight, the beginning of Sunday, September 16, when the blue-and-white Wartburg left the Bahrener Heights and returned to the town of Pössneck with Peter Strelzyk at the wheel. Peter Strelzyk was thirty-seven years old, a former aircraft mechanic; more recently a self-employed electrician; married, two children. Seated next to him was Günter Wetzel, a twenty-four-year-old bricklayer and truck driver, who was also married and had two children.

The two friends were quiet and pensive. Later they would comment that, driving past the familiar streets and buildings of their hometown, they were more mindful than usual of their surroundings. As they approached the town limits, the headlights picked up the words on a sign reading "Welcome to Pössneck". A while later they read the slogan on another sign, illuminated by a dim streetlight in front of the Socialist Unity Party district offices: "Go Forward Under the Banner of Marx, Engels, and Lenin."

There were no people on the streets at this time of night and very few cars on the road. Store windows had long since been darkened. But there was still activity behind the Hotel Posthirsch in the Café Dittmann. It was a Saturday night like any other and, as usual, youths in their late teens were dancing to the rowdy music of a rock band, this time one calling itself The Dance.

As they drove past Café Neubert in the marketplace, Peter Strelzyk was reminded that it was here, with the band playing "Dance with Me in the Morning" in the background, that he had first met a young apprentice by the name of Doris. They had now been married for almost sixteen years.

Passing the Gothic City Hall, Günter Wetzel reflected on his Socialist wedding to Petra Krause. "She wore an expensive white dress embroidered with flowers. In fact, our rings, gold-plated at thirty-five marks apiece, cost a lot less than the dress." Nearly six years had gone by since then. Their

The town limits of Pössneck, situated in the East German province of Thuringia. "Pössneck welcomes its guests," reads this highway sign. Pössneck, however, abhors the thought of its own citizens being guests of neighbourly West German towns.

son Peter was almost five years old, and little Andreas almost two. Later the two men were to find it strange that these things came to mind on this particular night.

This night would become a turning point in their lives. This was the night for which they had worked, sacrificed their money, and risked imprisonment: tonight they would gamble with their own lives, and those of their wives and children—they would attempt to escape with the wind to the West.

2

The Life
They Left
Behind

The wives and children waited impatiently in the den on the second floor for the men to return to the house at 22 Tuchmacher Street. To pass the time, they watched the movie *Angélique* on a West German television channel and later listened to the programme *Dance Until Midnight* on a radio station. According to the little quartz clock on the bookshelf, it was already twelve-thirty when the men finally returned from their drive.

Petra Wetzel made another pot of coffee, "none of that instant stuff, but real coffee, made from freshly ground beans from the delicatessen." The older children, fifteen-year-old Frank Strelzyk and his eleven-year-old brother, Andreas, drank tea. Peter Wetzel drank hot chocolate, and his little brother Andreas, still wide awake and energetic, was given thirty drops of a tranquillizer called Baldrian, mixed with warm sugar water to conceal its bitter taste.

The men calmed each other with encouraging words. "Actually, there's not much that can go wrong," said Peter. "If they catch us, then we'll all be sent to prison for a while, but then, before long, we'll be traded. They trade prisoners with West Germany for foreign currency all the time."

Both families were homeowners in Pössneck. They also owned cars, television sets, refrigerators, and washing machines. They ranked as members of the East German upper-middle class.

Aware that this was the last cup of coffee she would drink in the house on Tuchmacher Street, Doris Strelzyk pondered aloud, "Sometimes I wonder why we're willing to give all this up and take off into the unknown. Compared to others who are so much worse off than we are, we have a pretty good life here."

Her husband Peter, spokesman of the group, was already searching for the words he would use to explain to those on the other side why he had to leave. Eventually, he formulated his feelings in the following way: "We left because we wanted to live as free people and because we could no longer live as the property of a totalitarian regime. And because we were concerned about the future of our children . . ."

The majority of the more than 180,000 East German refugees who have registered in West Germany since the Berlin Wall was erected in 1961 gave similar reasons for defecting. Peter Strelzyk was not much different from others before him. He had no tangible reason for leaving; he was not an enemy of the state, nor was his life being threatened. He had, however, many vague motives, the accumulation of his thirty-seven years' experience as a citizen of East Germany. Over the years, the doubt he had felt as a young boy had developed into outright mistrust of those in power.

In spite of the fact that he had achieved a relatively high degree of wealth and security, feelings of discontent and disappointment overwhelmed him. He had become a pessimist, disheartened and frustrated, and responded with resentment toward the Party, the functionaries, and the entire authoritarian system. He began to lose control of his emotions and found it increasingly difficult to contain the anger within him. He described life in East Germany as "spiritual rape", robbing him of his freedom and dignity.

Peter Strelzyk was exactly thirty-seven years and one

month old on the day he left East Germany. He was nervous and tense, and even looked older than his age—rather like someone who already has stomach trouble and has to be careful not to develop an ulcer. The thin, dark beard made his face look haggard and pale, and drew attention to the dark shadows under his brown eyes and the well-defined creases near the corners of his mouth. He smoked too much: usually more than fifty Cabinett brand filter cigarettes a day. He was five feet nine inches tall, and slim—almost scrawny —at 141 pounds. "I may not be muscular, but I'm tough," he says, "and my body can take a lot."

A picture in the family album, taken only two years before, depicts a snappy young man with stylishly long hair, no beard, and a cheerful grin on his face. Peter had aged years in the meantime. He speaks quietly and thoughtfully, often pausing before answering questions, like one who's afraid of being misunderstood—or one who's accustomed to being listened to. He speaks softly, in a Thuringian dialect, and sometimes mumbles.

Peter Strelzyk was born in Oppeln on August 15, 1942, under the sign of Leo. After the war drove his family out of Upper Silesia, his father worked for the Construction Union in Gera, and the Strelzyks were constantly moving in an effort to find a new and better place to live. Consequently, he grew up in various Thuringian villages. After finishing school, Peter began an apprenticeship as a machinist in Pössneck and took electronics courses in his spare time. "I passed my exam as a qualified electrician," he says (using East German jargon to mean that he graduated from night school). At eighteen, the young technician was drafted into the National People's Army of the German Democratic Republic. "Actually, I wanted to be a pilot and signed up for the air force."

He was sent to aerotechnical school in Karmitz near Dresden, where he received training as a flight mechanic. Then, while repairing a fighter plane, he fell from a ladder and injured his lumbar vertebra; it still gives him trouble today. "That ended my dream of becoming a pilot. In 1963 I was released from the service as a flight mechanic and returned to Pössneck, where I found a position with People's Owned Polymer, a plastics and synthetic fibre factory."

Peter was ambitious and willing to work long, arduous hours to establish himself in his field. He was rapidly promoted to Foreman, took over as Efficiency Supervisor, and later was advanced to Department Head in charge of Automation Control Technology.

"I worked with an injection-moulding machine for sixteen years," he recalls. "Those machines have complicated control mechanisms, involving hydro- and electrodynamics." He enjoyed the work so much, and found the technical element of the job so intriguing, that he frequently went to work on holidays, even Christmas and New Year's Day, to repair defective machines.

"Sometimes the entire production run depended on me. They always gave me the most difficult problems, the most complicated repair jobs, the ones no one else could solve. Then I would sit there for hours, tinkering and pondering. I used to say to myself, 'You have got to make this damned Russian machine work again.' We had mostly Russian machinery, and it seemed that the more I swore at it, the quicker I could get it to function!"

As a result of his contributions to the factory, Peter received above-average wage increases. "The last few months before I left, I was sometimes earning 1,500 marks a month, a lot of money by East German standards." In addition, the incorrigible tinkerer was earning a small fortune through his ingenuity. He made numerous suggestions to speed up production, and executed them himself. For this, he received generous bonuses.

"I tried to find ways to modernize the completely antiquated production equipment. For instance, we had a moulding press with two manual levers, which was still operated by a worker. The operator had to push both of these levers to trigger the hydraulic mechanism that opened and closed the press. I rebuilt the thing so that it was fully automatic and the worker could be put to better use elsewhere."

Another piece of equipment had a built-in American

pump that was constantly on the blink. Even if spare parts had been available, they would have been prohibitively expensive, so Peter solved the problem by converting an East German pump (designed for entirely different purposes) to fit the specifications of this machine.

"That little idea saved the factory money in more ways than one. Not only did we save on parts, but on electricity as well, because (by contrast to the American pump) the East German pump could be regulated. Thanks to me, People's Owned Polymer saved 200,000 kilowatt hours that year." The Board of Directors awarded Peter three thousand marks, the highest premium ever paid for a single suggestion.

In all—and Peter Strelzyk is proud of this—he received more than 50,000 marks in bonuses. The ambitious technician was also commended in public when he was called before the assembled work force in the municipal civic centre and awarded "Recognition as an Activist in Socialist Emulation". On one such occasion, he even received the Medal for Outstanding Performance in his industry.

The plastics industry is considered a branch of chemistry and, traditionally, honours were bestowed on November 13, Chemical Workers' Day in East Germany. The most productive workers in the factory were summoned to the stage, which was decorated with flags, slogans, and flowers, while the other workers, decked out in their best suits, sat below in the audience and applauded.

Peter Strelzyk was on the stage so often that he can still recite the speeches from memory:

"Dear Comrades and Colleagues: Once again, it is that time of year when we feel it is our duty to single out, show our appreciation of, and honour the best workers among us."

"Dear Comrade Strelzyk: On the recommendation of your workers' collective, the factory management, the union management and the Party organization, you have again been selected for your exemplary performance in peaceful Socialist Emulation to receive Recognition as an Activist. With this certificate, please accept our sincere best wishes for the

continued success and happiness of yourself and your family. . . ."

After the speech, the district leader gave him two hundred
marks and a handshake; the union leader patted him on the
back; and the factory Board of Directors congratulated him.

Peter Strelzyk, son of a proletarian worker, had come far
in the First Workers' and Farmers' Republic of Germany.
According to the ideology of the State, he should have been
a happy Socialist—or at least a contented one.

His personal life had run as smoothly as his professional
life, and for that he was grateful. Peter Strelzyk, twenty-
three years old and just out of the service, was sitting one
day with friends in Café Neubert, a plush meeting place for
people of all ages. Little old ladies would come during the
week to enjoy the famous pastries and pies with their coffee
klatsches, while Peter's generation came at weekends to
drink beer.

On this particular Saturday, Peter noticed a small, shy girl
with large dark eyes sitting at the neighbouring table. "I was
immediately attracted to her and I found some stupid excuse
to speak to her. We talked about the weather and the music,
and then we danced."

Her name was Doris. She was barely sixteen years old and
was training to be an industrial salesperson. In her spare
time, she told Peter, she was a prompter at the new Pössneck
Workers' Theatre. The following day, Peter auditioned for
the role of the advocate in Molière's *The Imaginary Invalid*,
and from then on, he too worked at the theatre.

"Doris was such a terrific prompter," remembers Peter,
"that I hardly had to learn the text."

She jokes, "He wasn't a bad actor either, considering he
didn't have a speck of talent!"

Shadow of a Young Girl, by East German playwright
Rainer Krendl, dealt with Poland at the end of World War
II, and was the third and last production of the Pössneck
Worker's Theatre. "Most of the people either didn't have
time or were so involved in their jobs that the whole troupe
just slowly fell apart."

With the exception, that is, of Peter and Doris, prompter

and amateur actor. They remained together and were married in the Pössneck City Hall, symbolically on June 17, 1966, the Day of German Unity.

"We didn't go out of our way to be married on that particular day," says Peter, "but I was just beginning to take an interest in politics and somehow I thought that this date might be appropriately symbolic for our marriage."

Peter Strelzyk, pictured in 1962, in his East German Air Force officer's uniform. A gifted mechanic, Strelzyk for many years was fascinated by aviation, and he became the leader of the balloon escape.

Doris Strelzyk, pictured in 1958, at her First Holy Communion. She was married to Peter on June 17, 1966, ironically the thirteenth anniversary of the day in 1953 on which East German workers revolted to protest against authoritarian conditions in their country.

Café Karl Neubert in Pössneck, where Peter and Doris Strelzyk met in 1965. Open-air cafés like the Neubert dot towns and cities throughout East and West Germany.

3

The
Strelzyks

The Strelzyks' first apartment consisted of one room, six by ten feet, with a sink in it. The toilet was downstairs in the hallway. Their son Frank spent his first year in this tiny room while Peter ran from one agency to another, from the factory manager to the Party Headquarters to City Hall, trying to locate a larger apartment. His efforts were to no avail, and always met with the same excuse: "You aren't even a Party member, Mr. Strelzyk! There are many comrades ahead of you who are just as desperate for a larger apartment."

For the first time in his life, Peter "really got angry at those damned functionaries". Finally, no longer able to stand living with a wife and child in a "hole in the wall", he threatened to pitch a tent in the marketplace and live there with his family to show the townspeople of Pössneck how destitute his family was. He went to the local newspaper, *Volkswacht*, and announced his protest action. "A humourless, concerned man approached us there and told me that if I were to cause trouble, other authorities would take care of me—in other words, the State Security Service (Stasi)."

"They had been waving a Party registration form in front

of my nose all the time and I finally signed it." A few weeks later, the situation changed and the Strelzyk family was able to move to an attic apartment on Pössnecker Friedrich Engels Street. "It was a shambles," recalls Peter in disgust, "but it had a lot more potential than the other apartment." Three years later, in 1970, a larger apartment on the second floor became available. "Then I made it into a real luxury apartment (by East German standards). I wallpapered, installed a toilet, bath, and gas central heating, and was even able to get the old fireplace working again."

Four years later, the Strelzyks had their second son, Andreas. The apartment was too small now for a family of four with two active children, and situated as it was, directly on a heavily used main road, Doris was always worried when the children were outside playing.

In the meantime, Peter, high up on the ladder of professional success at People's Owned Polymer, was well paid and had good connections in the Socialist Unity Party. Now was the time to consider buying a house. He wanted something on the edge of town with a yard where the children could play. In 1975 he found what they had been looking for. It was an old house, built in 1930, but solid, and the location, Altenburg Circle, was ideal.

They bought the house from the Community House Management Committee, paying only 8,300 marks, which was the value of such houses in 1914. Peter explains, "In East Germany prewar houses are still sold at the old tax value. That makes buying property quite reasonable over there."

Peter obtained a home improvement loan and, with hard work and the help of friends, he turned the run-down building into a lovely home. New walls were constructed and a central coal-fired heating system, a new bath, and a new toilet were installed. Part of the cellar was converted into a garage with an inclined entrance. The remodelling took well over a year to complete because materials were so difficult to obtain. They waited weeks for wallpaper glue and years for bathroom tiles. There was a two-year delay for delivery of the bath, and the carpenter who offered to custom-make the door told them that it would be ready in two to three years.

In spite of the frustrations and problems involved, the Strelzyks were proud of their minor economic miracle. "Little by little, we filled the empty space: we bought a wall element for the living room, furniture upholstered in gold, red, and yellow, a stereo system, an a black-and-white television set." Peter covered the living room walls with insulated foam tiles. "They were expensive, 13.90 marks apiece, and I needed nine tiles per square yard for a total of nineteen square yards." To the left of the front door was a fireplace, the showpiece of the living room. "I redecorated it with white flagstone but, unfortunately, it wasn't functional and all we could do was look at it."

The Strelzyks had finally achieved a degree of prosperity and respectability. The bonuses Peter received for his suggestions at work and the four or five hundred marks a month Doris was earning as a senior clerk at Pössneck Savings Bank enabled them to buy a ten-year-old Moskwitsch automobile.

The street on which they lived, Altenburg Circle, is still considered a fine address in Pössneck. The neighbours, most of whom were dedicated Party comrades, were highly respected members of the small-town hierarchy: three members of the District Assembly lived in the houses on the left; the house across the street belonged to a former mayor; next to that lived a high functionary of the Free German Union Association. The People's Police Station was situated farther down the street, too close for comfort when they were building the balloon, and the manager of the People's Owned Polymer factory as well as the secretary of Pössneck's SED Party, who ran Peter's collective, lived right around the corner on Körner Street.

As is the custom in all Socialist countries, their children went to a day-care centre as infants, and later to a kindergarten. They attended the Ernst Thälmann School when they reached school age.

A cosy home, a well-balanced family life, success in his career—Peter Strelzyk had every reason to be content. But then he made a mistake—"a mistake to be avoided if one wants to come to terms with life in the German Democratic Republic."

He developed an intense interest in politics and began

comparing the theoretical Communist teachings of "freedom, equality, and brotherhood" with reality in East Germany. He searched unsuccessfully for a connection between the propagandist claims of "successful Socialist Emulation resulting in an ever-increasing standard of living" and the grim reality of daily life.

He came to the sorrowful conclusion that "the shower of propaganda was a pack of lies. In recent years things had got progressively worse instead of better. Even the most basic consumer goods were hard to find, prices had spiralled, and there was less freedom of thought and speech than ever."

Peter's doubts about the "repressive, regimented life in East Germany" bordered on despair. "Life became unbearable when I realized that I was being forced to live my life under the sanctions of the Party and that they ruled every aspect of my life."

As a member of the working population, Peter viewed conditions in East Germany differently to prominent intellectual critics such as Robert Havemann, Wolf Biermann, and Rudolf Bahro. Peter criticized the fact that the First German Workers' and Farmers' Republic was under the complete and absolute control of the Party. "What first disturbed me were the cheap propaganda lies, as deceptive as a black-and-white photograph—everything in East Germany was good and everything in the West was bad."

Peter brooded over memories of events from his past. "For example, in the early 1950s (I must have been ten or eleven years old) our teacher told us that the Americans had dropped potato bugs all over East Germany from aeroplanes to spoil our crops, and we were ordered to catch all these 'enemy bugs'." Peter later assumed that the story was fabricated by state functionaries to motivate the young pupils to work harder in the fields. The end effect, however, was that doubts were instilled in the children's minds as to the credibility of their teachers and officials.

Peter had another key experience while he was growing up: "I was an apprentice and had just received a new pair of blue jeans from the West, a valuable present which I proudly showed off to my friends. A group of us were stand-

ing in the Pössneck marketplace when several People's Police (Vopos) rushed toward us calling us rowdies, and
dragged us to the police station where they ripped the
Western brand labels off our jeans before releasing us."

In the late 1950s, the short, typically American crew hair-
cut was forbidden. A few years later, at the peak of the
Beatles' popularity, the Vopos rounded up long-haired
youths from all over town and set up chairs in the marketplace where two barbers cut their hair. "Although this was a
brutal demonstration of State authority, most of the spectators watched in silence," recalls Peter. When an elderly man
finally spoke up and said that he was reminded of Nazi
methods, he was chased away.

The mandatory assemblies, meetings, and Party rallies
had begun to annoy Peter when he was just in boot camp.
"It got to the point where I was practically allergic to words
like *objective, collective, brigade,* and *voluntary overfulfilment plan.* It may very well be," says Peter, "that Socialism
is an important concept in today's world, but in East Germany the word was so overused and misused that it left a
bad taste in my mouth."

After a while, Peter learned to live superficially as most of
his co-workers and friends did. He adapted to the situation
and made his way as best he could in the Socialist world in
which he lived. But just below the surface he harboured secret anger and cautious resistance.

It was his Socialist duty to attend, but he missed more and
more of the regular Party meetings which took place on
every second Tuesday of the month. "Once I walked out
when the Party secretary announced for the umpteenth time
that 'in order to meet the goals of Socialism and continue to
increase the prosperity of our Socialist population, it is necessary to further automate our production systems'."

When Peter stood on the Pössneck civic centre stage to
receive his Recognition as an Activist, he was embarrassed
by all the fanfare. "I knew as well as those in the audience
that this was nothing but a show of propaganda to spur
everyone on to even more overfulfilment and more hard
work. I felt like some kind of comic hero up there on the

stage and was ashamed to look my co-workers in the eyes."

In 1968, Peter Strelzyk and a handful of colleagues left a factory Party meeting in protest during a speech attempting to justify the invasion of Czechoslovakia by East German and Soviet troops.

He complained energetically to the factory management about poor working conditions which were endangering the health of the workers. "For example, six women had to sit in a windowless room where poisonous paint-thinner was stored." He was told that he was exaggerating and that nothing could be done to change conditions anyway. Eventually all six women were hospitalized for symptoms of poisoning.

Peter also had to go to hospital. "When my gallbladder had to be removed, the doctor told me in confidence that I had been breathing poison too long and that something should be done about the factory's inadequate ventilation system." Peter had suspected such dangers from the start.

He was furious each time the entire collective or brigade was asked to deliver a written "voluntary production goal" to the Party: "Dear Comrade Erich Honecker: This year the following workers at People's Owned Polymer pledge to . . ."

The Party also required that Party workers formally dissociate themselves from "enemies" of the working class, such as prominent East German intellectuals Wolf Biermann and Rudolf Bahro. "Most of us had never heard of Wolf Biermann, but we all had to sign a paper saying that we thoroughly disapproved of his behaviour. Later Rudolf Bahro's name was substituted for that of Biermann." Those who refused to sign were denied promotions, tourist visas to foreign Socialist countries, and new or larger homes.

In spite of Party promises of a higher standard of living in East Germany, the supply shortage became far worse than several years previously. A joke referring to the additional propaganda for the thirtieth anniversary of the Republic circulated in the summer of 1979: "A few years ago we were well off. Today we're better off than ever. We were better off when we were well off."

Thirty years after the war, socks and men's underwear were still hard to find, fish was an occasional treat, and high-

Peter Strelzyk, in a picture taken after the escape, thirty-seven years old.

Doris Strelzyk, in a picture taken after the escape, thirty-two years old. Lest the East German authorities believe she was an inferior homemaker, she insisted on making the family's beds and tidying up the house before the first escape attempt.

Frank Strelzyk, age fifteen. He, being the oldest of the four children, was the first to learn of the escape plans. Sworn to secrecy by his father, he helped in preparations for the balloon's takeoff.

Andreas, age eleven, the younger of the two Strelzyk boys. He sat restlessly through his school classes on one of the days when the family attempted to flee.

quality meat was a luxury. Building materials were often only obtainable by bribery and, even then, delivery sometimes took months or years.

Peter Strelzyk, a well-paid Recognized Activist, felt cheated. "The way I look at it, wages are supposed to reflect performance. If I try to buy something with my hard-earned money and can't get what I want, then I may as well have worked for nothing." He once asked a Party official why commodities that were so scarce in East Germany were so abundant in the West. Peter was astonished to hear that "the Capitalists only treat their workers so well so that they won't notice to what extent they're being exploited."

Peter, growing more and more discontented and despairing, buried himself in his work. Whenever possible, he avoided discussions in large groups and official meetings, including the more relaxed social evenings sponsored by collectives. "It was always the same empty, optimistic praise of the system. You could never be sure if the person standing next to you would report you to the police or, for that matter, worked for them. Consequently, no one dared express his honest, critical opinion."

The house on Altenburg Circle became an escape for Peter and his family from the regimentation of East German society. "At least within the walls of my own home I was free to do and say what I wanted." Peter noticed this same systematic retreat in many of his co-workers. "They closed the doors of their homes behind them and watched West German television in their living rooms."

The high television antennas on the roofs in the Thuringian town of Pössneck are all adjusted for West German reception. But while the townspeople enjoy Western television, the West German broadcasts are for many a constant source of torment and temptation. "It's like inviting a hungry man to a banquet and not allowing him to eat."

It must have been early in January 1975 when Peter first mentioned the possibility of escaping. "I can't remember what provoked me, but in any case, I asked Doris how she would feel about fleeing to the West."

"Have you lost your mind?" she replied. "Especially now

that things are finally beginning to go our way. And how would we manage with the children? Impossible!"

Peter Strelzyk wasn't so sure that escape was impossible. "I can't answer that yet," he said, "but where there's a will, there's a way. Whenever I make up my mind to do something, I find a way to do it. You know that as well as I do."

Assuming that her husband was joking, Doris shook her head and left for an advancement course at the Pössneck Savings Bank where she worked. But over the next few days, although she never mentioned it to her husband, she often caught herself reflecting on this conversation. "Peter's casual remarks made me think about the absurdity of our situation for the first time: less than eighteen miles from Pössneck there was another Germany, and we couldn't even go there because our own government forbade us to. We couldn't even go over there to compare the differences between here and there. Why not?"

Doris Strelzyk is a slim, well-groomed woman with black hair, very little makeup, a light shade of lipstick, and lightly plucked eyebrows. She often cut her own hair because "there was an unbelievably long waiting list for the hairdresser in Pössneck". Sometimes she made her own clothes, using patterns sent by acquaintances in the West. One of her main interests was the theatre. "I enjoyed participating in the Pössneck Workers' Theatre, but unfortunately it didn't last very long." She reads historical literature, particularly accounts of the peasants' wars, and is also an Edgar Wallace fan. Of all his detective stories, her favourite is *The Frog with the Mask*.

Doris had led a relatively quiet life in the East. Her father, a metalworker in the Max Hütte Steel Factory, placed her as a bank apprentice when she finished school, and later she found employment as a senior clerk with the Pössneck Savings Bank, where she was responsible for all personal bank accounts.

Although she enjoyed her job and got along well with clients and colleagues, she felt that she was underpaid. "I was earning two marks an hour, just enough to pay for a pack of cigarettes or half a pound of butter." She was too afraid to mention it at the time, but she particularly resented the fact that her male counterparts at the bank were earning almost twice as much for the same amount of work. "On the one hand there was constant talk of equality for East German women, yet, on the other hand, the man was automatically the 'main provider' who, as such, earned much more. I could never understand why bachelors were also considered family breadwinners who could command higher wages than women who were helping to support their families."

All things considered, though, Doris was satisfied with her life in Pössneck. Her children were nearly grown. Her older son Frank, technically adept like his father, was doing well in school and Doris was proud of his B average in mathematics and physics and C in Russian. He was on the Pössneck Advance handball team and a Blue Shirt member of the Free German Youth in the Magnus Poser group.

Her younger son Andreas had already completed the first phases of Socialist education, day-care centre and kindergarten. He was a fidgety child, much more excitable than his brother. His doctor attributed his nervousness to having been separated from his mother at too early an age. "Andreas had trouble concentrating in school," says Doris in the slightly critical tone of a concerned mother. "But concentration was no problem when he played forward wing on the Junior Pössneck Rotation soccer team."

The only thing that disturbed Doris about her life was that she could predict exactly what her future would be. She was a young woman who saw no opportunity for personal growth or change.

Every day of her life was exactly like the previous one. She awoke at 5:30 A.M., fixed breakfast, kissed her husband goodbye, and sent the children off to school. When Andreas was still in kindergarten she had had to push the pushchair more than a mile, often through rain, ice, and snow. She worked part-time at the bank, from seven to one, and often took courses in the afternoon. There was only one cinema in Pössneck (which showed films she never liked), the theatre had folded, and there were few places to go to dance in the evening. "So we usually just sat in front of the television set after dinner."

The Strelzyks spent their holidays close to home, drawing straws to decide between the Thuringian Forest or one of the nearby lakes. They had spent one holiday on the Baltic Sea but had never been to a foreign country. Plans to spend their holiday in Yugoslavia one year had to be cancelled because they were unable to obtain tourist visas.

The most unpleasant chore for Doris, as for most women living in the provinces of East Germany, was weekend shopping. "There were long lines of people waiting to get in the stores. Sometimes I had to wait for hours, especially at the fish and butcher shops, only to be told when it was finally my turn that they had just sold the last piece of what I wanted." Doris remembers, "Even the barest necessities were difficult to find, unless of course you had Western money, in which case you could buy anything your heart desired at the Hotel Posthirsch Intershop. But we never had Western money."

Doris gradually developed an interest in West Germany. She participated in intensive discussions at work about conditions there, and questioned West German visitors about their lives. She watched West German television with more awareness than before, and began tuning into the political and economic programmes as well as the quiz shows and movies. These same West German channels also showed scenes of the East-West border, of the high barbed-wire fences, the unploughed minefields and trip wires. "I was shocked when it finally dawned on me that all of this was only eighteen miles away from Pössneck, and I was reminded of the conversation with Peter about finding a way for us to escape to West Germany."

Doris often fantasized about a new life in the West, although the topic had not been mentioned for some time. "But," she admits, "I also wondered if I would be homesick for Pössneck. After all, I did grow up there and it was my home for many years."

4

"Let's All Strive Together"

Pössneck, the administrative centre of East Thuringia, 984 feet above sea level, with a population of 20,000, is primarily an agricultural town with some light industry. It is the home of the largest publisher of textbooks in East Germany, the Karl Marx Press, and famous for its Berggold chocolate.

The town nestles in a hilly area in central Germany, between the mountains of the Thuringian Forest on the southwest and the Leipzig lowlands on the northeast. Dark pine trees tower on the mountain range and corn ripens on the gentle slopes of the foothills below. It is here in the rich green valleys that healthy cows and hardworking farmers' cooperatives produce the dairy products that supply most of East Germany.

Most of the streets leading into town from every direction are paved with blue basalt from nearby quarries. The church steeple, visible from far away, is the town's main landmark. Also visible from a distance is the weathervane perched atop the Gothic City Hall, a building with elaborate gables and a covered pergola praised in travel guides as a sight worth seeing.

Pössneck in Thuringia, with its old marketplace, City

Hall, and church in the centre and its new housing projects on the outskirts, is almost identical to West German towns such as Buxtehude in Lower Saxony or Naila in Upper Franconia. Here, too, there's a river, a main street, a train station. The Orla River flows through Pössneck, emptying into the larger Saale River about a mile north of town. The main street is a thoroughfare leading to Jena and Weimar. Short-distance trains stop at Pössneck's antiquated station before continuing on to Saalfeld and Gera.

Pössneck's history can be traced back to 1252 when a colony settled on the banks of the Orla and called the area Peznitz. With the exception of the short time between 1806 and 1813 when Pössneck was occupied by the French, the town and its citizens have been fortunate and prosperous. The only disaster here occurred during the Thirty Years' War, when the plague took one thousand lives.

Present-day street names such as Gerbergasse (Tanner's Alley) and Tuchmacherstrasse (Clothmaker's Street) are reminders that earlier inhabitants were leather and textile craftsmen. According to the history books, they traded their wares with businessmen from as far west as Nuremberg and as far east as Leipzig.

Poets and chroniclers have little else to say about the tiny Thuringian town. Even Privy Councillor Johann von Goethe, at work in the nearby town of Weimar in 1800, had only one positive comment to make about Pössneck: "It seems to be a productive little town with a good council."

It was in Goethe's time that the fountain in the marketplace was erected with its statue of an armoured Pössneck citizen holding a shield and a lance, on which a dragon is impaled. Someone has knocked off a piece of the stone nose, but apart from that, it has suffered little damage over the years.

Pössneck was not much affected by World War II which was mainly fought farther north. The old houses are still standing, albeit desperately in need of renovation and fresh paint. The weathered facades resemble movie sets depicting small-town life in Germany in the early 1950s.

Westerners visiting Pössneck for the first time do, indeed,

have the feeling that the town has stood still since the post-war years. As in most East German provinces, traffic on the roads has not increased since the war, although the stench of double-exhaust cycles has worsened. Automobiles manufactured by Trabant, Wartburg, and Moskwitsch are reminiscent of the '40s and early '50s, as are the clothes of the people in the streets. Women wearing clumsy shoes and carrying large plastic shopping bags line up in front of the shops. Decorations in store windows are sparse and unimaginative. A delicatessen offering alcoholic specialities from foreign countries advertises "high spirits in friendly circles": Algerian red wine (9.50 marks) and Cuban rum (35 marks). The House of Ladies' Fashion presents the season's latest styles which rather resemble costumes from the movie *The Marriage of Maria Braun*—demure and timeless.

Pössneck, home of the Strelzyk and Wetzel families, is no place for automobile aficionados, gourmets, or fashion-conscious men or women. Here, the economic miracle never progressed further than children's shoes. But Pössneck is a charming, sparkling clean town. No paper litters the streets and, once a day, pigeon droppings are scrubbed off the flowerpots decorating the fountain in the marketplace.

Store windows and walls of buildings display more advertising for Socialism than for consumer goods. A sign in the window of the seafood store proclaims: "We strive with heart and mind to serve our customers and our Republic." An East German flag made of stiff paper, and a few greasy strips of smoked haddock fillet, apparently the only ware for sale on this particular day, lie next to the sign, seeming to contradict what Bertolt Brecht implied when he asked, "Which comes first, the soul or the stomach?"

Photographs of the "best activists" are plastered on the outside wall of People's Owned Rotasym, a ballbearing factory. On this particular day there were pictures of Manfred Schmetter (toolmaker) and Christel Kaschewski (toolmaker) from area F3 next to a large banner announcing: "Our goal—completion of our project in eleven months!"

The parabolic reflector antenna on top of the Socialist Unity Party building is always attuned to the capital of East

Berlin. A placard in the entrance of the building extols the "deepening friendship with the peoples of the Soviet Union".

The *Volkswacht* (People's Guardian), Party newspaper for the district of Gera, announces in its Pössneck edition that the municipality's model project in Socialist Emulation was once again successful, the printers at the Karl Marx Press having achieved fifty-three percent of the annual production goal within six months. "The printers accepted the Award for Outstanding Achievement in Socialist Emulation with pride and pleasure, and promised to honour the Republic's thirtieth anniversary by making every effort to achieve their pledge of 24.8 million books this year.

"In the race to fulfill the first stage of the Harvest Production Target, Complex II Oppurg is in first place, followed by Complex I Oppurg and Plough Complex Ernst Thälmann.

"As a result of the 'Let's all strive together!' action, 108,000 bricks and more than 49,000 roof shingles have been recovered for recycling from old buildings torn down between January and July of this year.

"The installation of a new heating system in the district Consumers' Cooperative has greatly improved working conditions. We are particularly grateful to engineers Hans Mathes and Louis Burghard, co-worker Alfred Hesse, bricklayer Tietze, and machinist Meinhard for their contributions to the project."

The local paper had the following comments to make on the thirty-fifth anniversary of the death of Ernst Thälmann, workers' leader and member of a Hitler resistance group: "Once again we mourn the day that Ernst Thälmann died at the hands of murderers. His spirit lives on and his ideas and ideals are still alive. . . . Laying of wreaths will take place at Ethel and Julius Rosenberg Place and at the Ernst Thälmann Monument on Neustädter Street. Buildings, streets, and other places named in his honour will be decorated with flowers."

On the editorial page, Hans Schmidt made a contribution to the eternal discussion as to what constitutes the working-class enemy, this time on the theme of "German Unity: An Illusion!" The author declared that "West German politicians have themselves destroyed unity. They are living in a dream world, on a cloud in the sky. Aren't they aware of the tremendous political reforms that have taken place on German soil? Are they not even aware of the most important change, the fact that the German Democratic Republic has been in existence for over thirty years?! Are they really blind to reality? The truth is they have no business here. The citizens of East Germany have asserted their right to choose for themselves, and have chosen the path of Socialism. It is senseless to talk of unity with the German Democratic Republic. Nothing can or should be changed."

Another day like any other in the Socialist East German town of Pössneck, eighteen miles from the border of East and West Germany.

An eighteen-year-old blonde in skin-tight faded Levis and a plaid blouse with the top three buttons undone sits on a bench in the marketplace smoking a Marlboro, presumably a present from someone in the West. The rest of the pack rests on her lap. She holds a copy of the glossy *West Fluppe* in her left hand and runs the fingers of her right hand through her boyfriend's hair. Behind the couple is a sign reading: "Eternal friendship with the Soviet Union; the land, its peoples, and Lenin's party."

The People's Owned factories and cooperatives close late in the afternoon in Pössneck. Collectives and brigades disperse and most, but not all, of the workers start home. Many have qualification courses on their schedules, further education in the form of evening courses offered by the factories. School children attend meetings, courses, or social gatherings organized by the Free German Youth. Every fifth Pössnecker borrows books from the People's Library. The town's athletic teams, Advancement and Rotation, boast more than three thousand members and offer complete programmes of soccer, handball, light gymnastics, swimming, and weightlifting. This year the town is proud that the women's handball team won the district trophy with a score of fourteen to twelve against the Gera Locomotives.

East and West German citizens do have one thing in common: most of the working class watches television when

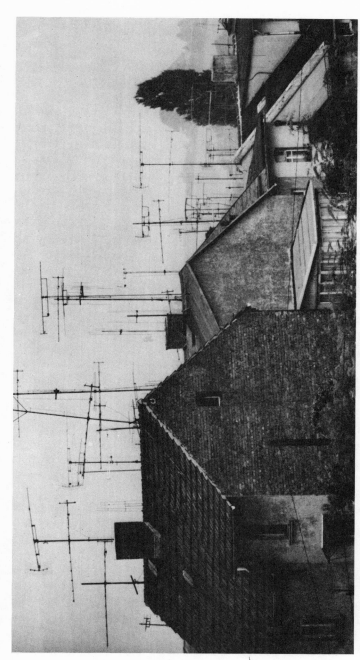

A view of the old houses which line a crowded street in Pössneck. The houses are dilapidated, but not their televisions—the forest of tall antennas testifies to the East Germans' intense need to pick up television reception from West Germany.

they come home in the evening and most of them, East and West, are tuned to West German channels. The personalities who appear in West German television advertisements, such as the Tschibo coffee taster in the commercial, are as well known in the East as in the West. An East German sociologist theorized to a West German journalist that "for many East German citizens, switching to a West German channel symbolizes a secret emigration of sorts to the West."

Many East Germans say that they seldom read the newspapers any more because of the long, tedious political commentary. If they read the paper at all, they look at the classified section in search of job offers: "The Personnel Department of Wismut Mining is looking for applicants to fill surface and below-ground positions important to the economy."

Court sentences are publicly announced in the papers: "The regional court of Gera hereby notifies the people of Thuringia that transportation worker Klaus P. and pipestock tapper Hans Jürgen G. have been sentenced to two years and six months imprisonment, respectively, for first-degree robbery."

In the used trading column there are offers of manual drills, Biedermeier-style sofas, antique vases, and used wedding dresses (light blue, worn only once, 130 marks). A discreet mailing house in Dresden offers Mondos prophylactics at three dozen for twelve marks. An amateur gardener is in the market for a small plot with a shed. (For years, garden allotments have served the lower class in and around Pössneck as a flight to a private idyllic world.)

The Greizer Symphony is playing Bach and Beethoven at the Civic Centre, and brigade cabarets allow themselves the pleasure of satirical digs at officials. Rock bands play dance music for Pössneck's youth.

At Café Dittmann an orchestra is playing a different kind of dance music this weekend. Guests have to order at least a split of German champagne, or a beer and a schnapps. This is a favourite meeting place for the more volatile southerners from Algeria, "guest workers" in Pössneck's factories. More often than not, there are fistfights between the southern "guests" and their northern hosts, forcing the People's Police to intervene. And every travelling salesman knows that "Café Dittmann is the place to find a nice date, someone who wouldn't mind earning fifty marks on the side—West German marks, of course."

Western visitors to Pössneck (or anywhere else in East Germany) find it difficult to find East Germans who are willing to talk openly. Mistrust and scepticism of the "conceited Westerners who just want to show off their new cars" is widespread, as is the fear that "a district functionary might be sitting at the next table". Relaxed discussions take place only in private homes where contact has been made through mutual friends.

A West German journalist recently held such a discussion with four young people from Pössneck (two students at Halle University, an employee from a publishing house, and a young mother). All four East Germans were intelligent and alert and gave their honest opinions about living conditions and the economies in East and West Germany.

All four found it very important not to belong to the Party. One of the students explained, "I would rather think for myself and I think most young people in East Germany feel the same way." He added, "I'm sure there's a lot to criticize about the East German State and its particular brand of Socialism, but times have changed and not everyone would cross the border to West Germany even if given the opportunity." The other student said, "Here at least we know that we will find work after graduation. I understand that's not always the case in West Germany."

When asked about the continual negative comparisons made between the economies of East and West Germany, all four answered by quoting Erich Honecker, Chairman of the Council of State of the German Democratic Republic: "Where would your distinguished Capitalist gentlemen be today if West Germany had started with only the four steel factories that we were left with in 1945, instead of the 120 that they had?"

One of the students added, "Granted, they do earn more than we do, can buy more for their money, and everything they want is available. But we aren't exactly starving either. And three out of four families have refrigerators, washing machines, and television sets. Every fourth family even has a car."

"Where did you get your information?"

"From official sources." Defensively, he added, "But it's obvious anyway. All you have to do is look around." And he pointed to the television set and refrigerator.

"What is it that you like about the German Democratic Republic?"

These young, politically minded people answered unanimously, "Here we have no more exploitation or Capitalism."

"But doesn't the Party use the State apparatus to exploit the people?"

"Of course, it's true that too much of the surplus value remains in the hands of the Party and bureaucracy. There are many complaints to be made against the State functionaries, but at least they aren't putting the money in their own pockets like those in private business in the West. Most of the money here is invested toward the well-being of the people as a whole."

He added, "But this constant pressure, this never-ending push toward overfulfilling the plan, and the whole spectacle of Socialist Emulation, gets to be too much sometimes."

The first student said, "We should keep more of our products here where they're needed and not export so much. The Russians seem to think we're Santa Claus or something."

Toward the end of the discussion, the most talkative of the students said, "We're Socialists in principle but we are aware of the problems. We too would like to be able to say what we really think, even if those in power don't approve of what we have to say. We desperately need people like Bahro and Biermann here. And what they're doing to Havemann . . . well, it's inexcusable!"

Mention of the Wall in Berlin, and the national border with the West, evokes anger in these loyal but critical East German citizens.

The young woman, who had only nodded or shaken her head until now, expressed herself for the first time: "My family and home are here and I feel that this is where I belong. I don't think that I would enjoy living in the West. But I would like to see for myself what life's like on the other side—just to go there and talk to the people and then come back here."

Another of the young Socialists interrupted, "And if I should then decide that I would rather stay there, I would like to be free to do so."

This conversation took place a short time ago in an East Pössneck apartment, part of a modern project on the edge of town housing four to five thousand people, most of them young families. While the project was under construction, there was a rumour going around that a particularly inefficient construction brigade had installed prefabricated kitchen walls with serving windows in the bathrooms by mistake.

"That's our idea of rationalization, East German style," one of the workers is supposed to have said. "Here you can sit on the toilet and eat your breakfast at the same time. The new tempo is Socialist Emulation!"

5

The
Wetzels

Peter had had many discussions about life in East and West Germany. He says, "It was always a torture for me because each discussion made me more and more aware that I had somehow ended up on the wrong side of the German border. I began to yearn for life in the West, for freedom of thought, freedom to go where I wanted, and for the possibility to grow and develop as an individual. I wanted to be somewhere, anywhere, where I wasn't under constant pressure to be like everyone else.

"The idea of escaping had started out as just a game I played with myself, but the desire to do something about it grew. On the other hand, the more I thought about it, the more convinced I was that I couldn't do it alone. I would need help."

In the summer of 1973, Peter met someone who might be able to help him. Anneliese Hoffmann, an old friend of Doris's, was visiting Pössneck from West Germany. Anneliese and her second husband had many ties with Pössneck. She had grown up there, married her first husband, and had given birth to her daughter Petra. Later she had divorced her husband and emigrated to West Germany when it was still easy, before the Wall was erected. Petra had remained behind with her father to be raised by a foster-mother. Unable to get a tourist pass for several years, Anneliese didn't see her daughter again until much later.

So it happened that on a sunny weekend in 1973 the Strelzyks met their friend Anneliese Hoffmann and her eighteen-year-old daughter, Petra Krause. Petra brought along her shy, young boyfriend, Günter Wetzel, who shared Peter's interest in anything mechanical or motorized.

Peter recalls that they spent that first afternoon talking about mopeds, motorcycles, and cars, and that Günter showed great interest in the machines Peter spent most of his time repairing at the factory. In spite of the age difference between the two men, a strong friendship developed. Günter helped repair his new friend's car and cheerfully helped the Strelzyks with the house renovation.

Peter and Doris attended Günter Wetzel and Petra Krause's wedding on February 14, 1974, at the Pössneck City Hall, and watched as an official placed the cheap rings on the fingers of the nineteen-year-old bride and groom and handed them the green imitation-leather "family book".

The bride wore a white dress with embroidered flowers and a shoulder-length veil covering her face. She had white daisies in her hair. The groom was dressed in a dark suit with a spray of white lilies-of-the-valley peeking from his breast pocket. A white bow tie at his neck softened the stiff lines of the starched white shirt. It was obvious from the pink glow of his cheeks that he spent much of his time outside in the fresh air. He was of average height, stocky, strong, with muscular forearms and large hands—a quiet, shy young man who describes himself in these words: "Sometimes I get really annoyed with myself because I don't find it easy to make friends. But at other times I like myself because I'm a calm person who doesn't get upset easily."

Günter's family background is almost as complicated as that of his young wife. In Günter's case, it was his father who left the family when Günter was still a child to emigrate to the West. Günter spent his school years with his mother in the village of Grobengereuth near Pössneck. "In retrospect, it was a happy childhood. Country children have so much more freedom than city children."

He was a poor student, shy and introverted in the classroom. But he was clever enough to build his first radio when he was ten years old. Two years later he rebuilt an old discarded Star moped which he proudly rode through the fields and villages. Later he repaired motorcycles for neighbours in the village.

The budding young mechanic couldn't have cared less about politics. "At the time, I don't think I was even aware of the fact that we were living in a divided country, or that Grobengereuth was only a few miles from the border."

He was introduced to East-West politics purely by chance. In 1965, while he and some classmates were helping with the potato harvest, he tripped over a strange object in a furrow. "There was this bundle on the ground with a timer attached and a package in it. Not knowing what it was, I stuck it in my pocket and took it with me."

When he got home, he opened the package and found a brochure entitled *Where Would You Rather Live?* This was one of the many West German propaganda pamphlets sent from Bonn by what was then called the Ministry of Internal German Affairs to German citizens in the Soviet Occupation Zone. During the Cold War, propaganda pamphlets and books were attached by the West German border police to small helium balloons and, when the wind was right, sent soaring in the direction of the border. A timer triggered the release of the packages, and the material was strewn over East German territory. Dozens and sometimes hundreds of flyers were distributed in this way.

It was one of these packages that young Günter Wetzel had found. "When I showed my treasure to my friends they told me that it was inflammatory material and should be turned over to the police. That aroused my curiosity enough to make me read the book."

The book compared life in East and West Germany and was full of boring statistics on wages and prices. But Günter also read about the prosperity in West Germany and that it was possible to buy all different makes of automobiles there.

That did it! Günter Wetzel was interested in the East-West situation from that time on. The efforts of the propagandists in Bonn had been successful, and Günter kept the little pamphlet for many years.

Günter left school at fourteen after completing the eighth grade. "My grades were getting progressively worse because I wasn't interested in what they were teaching. I guess I have to admit that I was lazy too, and never studied."

His poor grades ruled out the possibility of an apprenticeship as a truck mechanic as he had hoped, but he was able to find a trainee position with People's Owned Pössneck Construction as a bricklayer. For three years he worked with brick and mortar helping other apprentices build the "first Socialist State on German soil", constructing new housing projects such as that in East Pössneck. In the process, he developed wide shoulders and strong arms, and he joined the Pössneck Rotation sports organization where he went regularly at weekends to lift iron weights weighing hundreds of pounds.

"I had planned to go back and finish school after my apprenticeship so that I could be an auto mechanic." But then he met someone who made him forget his ambition.

On a hot summer day in 1973, carrying a friend on the pillion seat of his rebuilt motorcycle, he rode to a pond hidden in the hills above Pössneck. Thinking they were alone, they dived into the cool water of the tiny, idyllic lake surrounded by woods and played around in the manner of teenage boys, until they discovered a girl fishing on the opposite bank.

"And that's how she caught me," says Günter, grinning.

The girl with the fishing rod recalls, "At first I was angry because I really had wanted to catch some carp and the two of them had scared all the fish away. So I yelled at them to go away. But I guess I didn't sound very convincing because I was glad to have the company. Anyway, they swam up and sat down next to me."

Günter flirted with the young girl who explained that she was spending a summer holiday on the lake with several adults. They were camping on the edge of the woods. When the two men finally said goodbye, the girl hinted that she could usually be found fishing on the bank of the lake.

Günter returned the following day without his friend, pretending that he had lost his keys. But, face to face with the girl again, he was suddenly shy and unsure of what to say. It was she who finally took the initiative and started to tell him about herself.

In the weeks and months that followed these tentative conversations, Günter and Petra got to know each other very well and fell in love. A year later, they were married in the Pössneck City Hall and Petra Krause, Anneliese Hoffmann's daughter, became Günter Wetzel's wife.

Petra's foster-mother, who planned to emigrate to West Germany as soon as she reached retirement age, signed over her house on Tuchmacher Street as a wedding present to the young bride.

Günter recalls, "The old house was practically falling apart but we were grateful for it. We started working on it immediately to fix it up. Being a bricklayer, I was able to do most of the work myself."

Günter had changed jobs frequently since his apprenticeship, and each new job was better than the last. He had worked for the Reconstruction Cooperative in Pössneck for a while as a machine operator where he discovered that he had not outgrown his love of motors and machines. Then he had worked for the Inter-Union Forest Agency Cooperative in Orlatal as a push-tractor driver. Here his job was to pull sawed-off tree stumps out of the ground with a tractor and transport newly felled Thuringian pine trees to the lumber mill in a truck.

"But I still knew how to repair automobile engines and power saws. Something was always malfunctioning and I enjoyed fixing things, even though I still had had no formal training as a mechanic."

Two years later, Günter was hired by People's Owned Trucking and Transport in Saalfeld. Often travelling for days at a time, he drove the so-called "furniture suitcase", a Skoda truck, all over East Germany delivering furniture from Thuringian factories to stores anywhere between Rostock in

Petra and Günter Wetzel, both nineteen years old, at their wedding on February 14, 1974. Close friends of the Strelzyks, they helped Peter and Doris renovate their home before collaborating on the balloon escape.

Günter Wetzel, in a picture taken after the successful escape, twenty-four years old. While never much of a student, he had a gift for mechanics.

Petra Wetzel, in a picture taken after the escape, like her husband, only twenty-four years old. She was the most reluctant of the balloon plotters and was plagued by recurring nightmares of an ill-fated flight.

Petra, pictured with her two young sons, five-year-old Peter and two-year-old Andreas, in the family's adopted town of Naila in West Germany.

the north and Leipzig in the south. "Sometimes I worked as many as 270 hours a month and only got between nine hundred and one thousand marks for my labour."

Günter Wetzel was a hardworking man. At weekends, and whenever possible in the evenings during the week, he worked on his own house on Tuchmacher Street. He and Petra renovated the old house from cellar to attic.

Although progress was constantly delayed because of difficulty in obtaining building materials, they were still able to install a central gas heating system, build a new chimney, add walls, and lay a new roof. The narrow, three-storey house, wedged between two similar houses built in the same period, was larger than it appeared from the outside.

They furnished a large living room, a kitchen with a breakfast nook, a master bedroom, and two children's rooms. There was still one room left over on the first floor for Günter to make into a workshop. "We had borrowed 25,000 marks for renovation and that much money goes a long way in East Germany."

They had no trouble getting the loan because both of them were working at the time. Petra, too, was ambitious, and advancing quickly in her job at the People's Owned Tool factory in Pössneck where screws, clamps, boring bars, and other tools were manufactured.

Neckermann, one of West Germany's largest mail-order department stores, was the factory's main customer. "We manufactured a special Type SB-3 drill just for them and spray-painted them bright yellow as requested. No one ever bothered to make tools attractive for the East German consumer."

Petra was promoted from a simple assembly-line worker to the middle-management position of quality controller. It was her job to determine if the work of her co-workers was up to the norm. "If the work didn't meet set standards, I sent it back for improvement. Or sometimes, if it were really bad, I would just throw it out."

Petra was good at her job, a sociable person with a pleasant sense of humour. She readily earned the respect and friendship of male co-workers and subordinates.

"Actually, I had wanted to be an artist originally," says

Petra, who has recently started painting landscapes and still lifes. In school she had also been a good athlete and once won the Pössneck swimming championship in breaststroke. "A team doctor examined me and found that I had more than average lung capacity and that my heart was fifty percent larger than average. That probably explains why I was so successful in sports."

Petra's happiest memories are of the holidays spent on Lake Mal at the edge of the Thuringian Forest. "We went camping there, and spent our time fishing and picnicking on the banks. When it was hot we would swim in the lake and we'd get up early in the morning to pick mushrooms in the woods. When the weather was nice, it was heavenly there."

As a teenager, Petra loved to dance. "I would get together with friends to go to the Free German Youth dances held at the Civic Centre. Or we would spend our afternoons in the dance cafés in Pössneck."

She wore the short miniskirts and tight hot pants that were the latest fashion in East Germany as well as in the West. Smoking was "in" too, so she puffed up to twenty Old Jewel cigarettes a day. An avid collector of rock music records, her most valuable possession was a double LP of an Elvis Presley concert that her mother had brought along on one of her infrequent visits from the West.

"You can't imagine what it meant to me. A record like that would have cost several hundred marks on the black market in East Germany."

Petra had wanderlust occasionally. "Especially when my stepsister, who lived in West Germany, sent me postcards from her holidays. Cards arrived from everywhere—Italy, Spain, Greece, once even from Africa! I remember looking at the picture of the Pygmies on one of the cards and wondering if I would ever have a chance to travel to such exotic countries." Unfortunately, Petra never got to travel. "Until I married Günter, the farthest I had been was a school trip to Berlin."

And once she was married, other things became more important. Renovation of the house she had inherited was given first priority, and she delighted in decorating it according to her own taste.

"We bought a large bookshelf made of chipboard with a brown veneer and white shelves." Presents from the West, an expensive quartz clock and a large Cognac decanter, decorated the shelves. Even the bedspread in the master bedroom and the wallpaper with the animal design in the nursery, which was ready and waiting long before their first son was born, came from West Germany.

Petra and Günter tell about the birth of their first son: "It was a difficult delivery, a high-risk pregnancy from the very beginning, and when complications arose, the doctor had to force labour." Hospital personnel insisted that the nervous father-to-be should go home and calm down.

Instead, Günter went to work and was assigned a long haul that took him away for two days. "I returned to find a telegram announcing that Petra had given birth to my nine-pound, twenty-one-inch son Peter."

Petra, a heavyset woman with reddish-brown hair and grey-green eyes, gave birth to their second son Andreas three years later. "I gained more weight with each pregnancy and each time it was harder to lose."

Petra talks hurriedly and emphasizes her words with jerking hand movements. About herself she says, "I consider myself a cheerful and sociable person, a complement to my husband, who's a quieter type."

She had never paid much attention to politics, but there were two things that had always disturbed her about East Germany: "The people who did understand what was going on were afraid to say what they thought. That bothered me. And no one was allowed to leave the country to travel. That bothered me too."

By the time she was twenty-four years old, Petra Wetzel—working woman, wife, and mother of two—sometimes felt that she had taken on too much responsibility too soon.

"I'm afraid of two things," she says, "getting old and going to the dentist, in that order. I'm one of those women who would have liked to remain a teenager forever."

When asked what it is that she loves the most, she answers, "I love my children and my husband, but, most of all, I love life."

6

===

Planning
the
Escape

The casual relationship between the Strelzyks and Wetzels quickly developed into deep friendship based on common problems and interests. Petra and Doris, both working mothers, exchanged experiences and advice about how to cope with careers and young children. The families took turns visiting each other, and Günter and Peter would drink Pössnecker Rosenbräu beer while they discussed cars and engines. When all four of them got together, the main topic of conversation was the joys and suffering involved in renovating old houses.

Working together as one team on both houses, they found that they were able to accomplish much more than alone. In his spare time, Günter used the People's Owned truck to deliver gravel and shingles to the Strelzyks' house on Altenburg Circle. In return, Peter assisted with the installation of the Wetzels' new heating system in their house on Tuchmacher Street.

The true test of friendship came with a bath shortage. Peter explains, "My bathroom was almost finished. I wanted to buy a bath for it but couldn't find one for sale anywhere. I was terribly disappointed. Then Günter told me that, in anticipation of a shortage, he had bought one earlier. But now that he had it, he couldn't use it because he was still waiting for tiles and bathroom fittings. So he gave me his bath! He didn't get his fittings until a few months later. By that time, my bath had arrived and I passed it on to him."

It was friendly gestures such as this one that made it easier to deal with the everyday frustrations of life in East Germany and also formed a binding friendship between the two very different men. Eventually, they felt that they trusted each other enough to air their opinions about the economic and political situation in the German Democratic Republic.

Günter, the frustrated mechanic, says, "Sometimes it almost drove me crazy at work! A large truck would go unused for months simply because a stupid cylinder-head gasket that only cost 14.30 marks couldn't be found anywhere in southern East Germany. The result, of course, was a tremendous decrease in production. But there remained all this talk about the success of Socialist Emulation. None of it was true. Our company would have been bankrupt long ago by Western standards. Sometimes it was no fun working there."

The two men discussed current events. They learned from West German television that Wolf Biermann, East German singer and critic, had been exiled. Later they learned about retaliation against Robert Havemann and that in the neighbouring town of Rudolstadt a group of political critics had been sentenced in a secret trial to long-term imprisonment.

West German television also broadcast news about the sentence that Rudolf Bahro received for the ideas he expressed in his latest book, one that Peter felt had been written in an effort to improve conditions in the German Democratic Republic.

Peter says, "We discussed the Bahro case in detail and agreed that the dictatorship of the proletariat in East Germany had long since become a dictatorship of functionaries, and that individual freedom was being reduced more and more."

Günter too had developed an interest in the political and

social situation in East Germany. "When we watched people on West German television criticizing the government, we felt uncontrollable envy. Such honesty was out of the question where we lived. We felt like second-class citizens in comparison to the West Germans."

A shopping trip to East Germany's capital had a lasting effect on Petra and Günter Wetzel. They were there to buy a warm water mixer for the house (impossible to find near Pössneck) and decided to use the opportunity to get to know Berlin a little better. Strolling along the streets, engaged in window-shopping, they suddenly found themselves staring at the Wall dividing the city into East and West.

Petra says, "I wasn't very well informed about what had led up to the division of Germany or why the Wall had been erected in the middle of Berlin. I stood there, completely unprepared, with this ugly grey Wall in front of me. I saw the barbed wire and the patrol towers, watched the armed soldiers walking back and forth, and was reminded of scenes from prison films I had seen on television. From somewhere deep inside, I felt anger I had never known before. I asked Günter how it was possible for our own government to lock us in behind the Wall, but he didn't answer me."

It was several minutes before either of them spoke. But they were both thinking the same thing. For the first time, they thought about fleeing to the West. Petra says, "The idea of escaping came to me spontaneously—in spite of the fact that we were in the middle of rebuilding our house and everything. But I forgot about it after a few days because I knew that there was no way to escape."

However, this was a turning point for Petra. It opened her eyes to what was happening in her country and the world around her. She suddenly saw bitter irony in the Socialist slogans plastered around her hometown. She found the sign in front of the Party headquarters—"Go forward under the banner of Marx, Engels, and Lenin"—particularly distasteful. And she returned from Berlin to find that suddenly the houses in Pössneck seemed just as colourless and depressing as the area near the Wall in Berlin.

Routine inconveniences that she had accepted as a matter

of course, such as waiting in line for hours in front of the shops, now made her angry. She realized for the first time that none of her friends said what they were thinking.

"Almost everyone complained in private conversations about conditions in East Germany, but publicly, or even within a circle of co-workers, no one dared mention the deplorable state of affairs. Even political jokes were rarely told because everyone was afraid of the Secret Police. I felt as if I were living in a giant prison."

When her mother visited from West Germany, Petra felt envy and resentment. "I realized that over there they had everything that we were denied. They could go anywhere they wanted. They could curse the regime as loudly and as often as they wanted. And they could buy almost anything they wanted if they worked hard enough."

Eventually, she came to the conclusion that life in East Germany was unjust. She searched for answers and explanations. "Why do the functionaries make all the decisions and plans? Is it true that everything is done with the welfare of the people and citizens in mind? How long do we have to wait to see this 'better future and prosperity' they promise us? Why doesn't the individual citizen see progress if what they say is true? It's all propaganda."

All of this is only part of the reason why people like Petra and Günter Wetzel want to make a break for freedom and escape to the other Germany. Petra says, "Everyone, no matter where he is, has an urge to do something crazy once in his life, something forbidden by the law, or the Party, or the financial advisor. I had a crazy wish too. I would have liked to go somewhere really fancy. I wanted to do myself up like other young women do, maybe wear a big Afro wig and hoop earrings. But those things wouldn't be available in Pössneck for another ten years."

While Petra fantasized, Günter and Peter found other ways of coming to terms with their situation. Peter Strelzyk, Party member and twice recipient of an Activist Award, defied the officials and quit his job at People's Owned Polymer to start his own business as an electrician in Pössneck, even though he didn't have an official trade licence. At first,

Günter helped out part-time, and later on a full-time basis. They made plans to form a partnership someday—if not in East Germany, then in the West.

They were so much more dependable and efficient than state electrician services that they quickly built up a large clientele which kept them busy laying wiring and repairing appliances in private homes, apartments, and even in small state factories.

While they worked, they had serious discussions about the political situation. Peter confided to his friend that he had made plans in 1975 to flee the country. "I wanted to take the family to Yugoslavia on holiday and planned to escape from there to Austria. The whole thing fell through because we were denied tourist visas."

Günter and Peter made a game of trying to come up with safe and easy ways to get out of East Germany without getting caught or killed. They came to the conclusion that it was practically impossible to escape by the land route, which was hermetically sealed by mines and guards. And since there was no water on the border near Thuringia, the only way to get out was by air. "But where in the hell were we going to get an aeroplane or helicopter?"—not to mention the fact that neither of them knew how to fly one.

One day, one of them came up with a scheme. Neither knows who mentioned it first, but they do remember exactly when and where the idea started to take shape. It was March 7, 1978, the day before the official Women's Day in East Germany.

They had just finished a job at People's Owned Apolda, a leather-processing plant in Neustadt on the Saale River, and were sitting down to lunch when one of them said, "Listen, I have an idea. Why don't we build ourselves a balloon?"

Both of them were fascinated by the idea from the very beginning. It was so farfetched that they were sure it would work. No one, not even the East German Security Service, would believe that a balloon could possibly provide a viable means of escape.

They continued working on the new electrical switches they were installing, but their enthusiasm for the project was gone. From that moment on, the very purpose of their lives changed.

Peter says, "All of a sudden, we had a goal—an entirely different outlook on the future. Vague talk of escape had become more than just talk. Now there was hope. We had come up with a possible way to escape East Germany."

Günter adds, "Of course, the technical challenge made the idea even more attractive. Neither of us had the slightest idea how hot-air balloons actually worked."

That evening the two men sat together in the Wetzels' living room and drank several glasses of Nordhäuser Korn, an East German schnapps, and imagined themselves already "up, up, and away" in a homemade balloon.

They did understand the basic principle of the hot-air balloon. That hadn't changed in the two hundred years since the French Montgolfier brothers had built the world's first balloon. "We knew, of course, that hot air rises. So basically all you had to do was heat the cold air in the balloon with some sort of flame strong enough to produce the heat necessary to push the balloon, gondola, and passengers to the sky."

The next morning they went to the Peoples' Library in the Pössneck marketplace, looking for information. They found nothing specific about balloon technology, but they did find a book entitled *The Technology of Gas-Fitting*. And Peter read from the *Brockhaus Encylopaedia of Physics* under the heading "Montgolfier": "Montgolfier, brothers. Inventors of the hot-air balloon. . . . They conducted experiments in their father's paper mill using paper bags filled with smoke. . . . On June 5, 1783, the first unmanned hot-air balloon, called a Montgolfière, ascended. It was made of canvas, lined with paper, and covered with a hemp net. The air in the balloon was heated from the open bottom by glowing charcoal in a cup. In September 1783, a Montgolfière with animal passengers was sent up and landed safely. . . . The first human flight in a Montgolfière took place on November 21, 1783, near Paris, under the direction of J. F. Pilatre de Rozier and the Marquis D'Arlandes. The balloon was 3710 cubic yards in size. . . ."

Peter handed the book to Günter and whispered, "Good

Lord, Günter, if they could do it two hundred years ago, we should be able to do it today."

When they reached home, the bricklayer and electrician began their first calculations and sketches for the classic aircraft. Peter found that some of the knowledge he had accumulated during his short stint as an aircraft mechanic came in handy. "Like how to calculate the cubic capacity of the balloon and the dynamic lift necessary to push a given weight. . . . I knew right away that, theoretically, I would be able to figure the whole thing out, at least on paper."

The balloon would have to carry eight people (four adults and four children), plus the weight of the gondola, the heating system, and the fabric of the balloon itself. "All told, we figured the total weight would be around 1,700 pounds."

Using the isobaric equation for the state of air, they added, multiplied, and divided until they finally arrived at the amount of material they thought they would need for a balloon large enough to carry the weight. They figured they would need at least 2,600 cubic yards of fabric.

In other words, the balloon would have to have the capacity to hold as much air as a large house. They would also have to find a way to heat the air in the balloon to at least 212 degrees Fahrenheit and to maintain that temperature long enough to get them from their point of departure in East Germany across the border to West Germany, a distance of about eighteen miles. Assuming ideal wind conditions, they estimated that it would take them at least thirty minutes in the air to reach the other side.

Although they realized the complexity and enormity of the undertaking, Peter and Günter were not put off. "The most immediate problem was how and where to get enough material for the balloon itself, and the other raw materials for the gondola and burner system."

Before they could begin, though, they had to inform their wives of the scheme. Doris Strelzyk was not at all surprised when Peter informed her of the wild idea at dinner. "I knew that Peter had solved all kinds of problems at the factory. Why shouldn't he be capable of figuring out a way to build a hot-air balloon? It sounded risky to me but I knew I could

The forty-year-old Gritzner sewing machine that was used to patch together the enormous balloon. Representatives of the West German Singer Sewing Machine Company, mistakenly believing that the machine had been an old Singer model, offered each family a new Singer in a promotional gesture. When the truth surfaced, the offer was rescinded.

trust Peter's judgment. And anyway, the whole thing sounded so improbable that deep down I secretly thought that it was probably just a pipe dream after all. I wasn't going to worry about it yet."

The Wetzels, still in the process of remodelling their house, had recently bought a Russian Raduga television set. Günter had a difficult time explaining to Petra why he had chosen this particular time—when they were finally beginning to get all the things for which they had strived so long —to talk of leaving.

Petra remembers how he told her. They had just finished dinner. Petra was about to clear the table when Günter brought two glasses and a bottle of wine over.

"Don't get up yet, Petra. I have something important to talk to you about."

"What is it? Why are you so serious?"

Günter hesitated, choosing his words carefully before he spoke. "We're both still so young and have so much time left to enjoy life. Do you think we can get the most out of life if we have to spend the rest of our lives here in East Germany? I don't! Look what's happening around us. Things are getting worse. Let's get out of here. We're young and intelligent and it would be so easy for us to start over in the West. I know it's not exactly paradise over there either. We'd have to work just as hard there to have the things we want. But we're used to hard work. And anyway, life would be different there. We could do all the things we've always dreamed of doing. We could go wherever we wanted—Italy, Spain! You name it! But most important, Petra, we have to consider our children and their futures. More than anything, I want them to grow up in a free country."

Petra was silent for several minutes. She was apprehensive and worried about the risks involved, but she kept her fears to herself. Finally she said, "You decide what's right for you. If you think that we'd be happier in the West, then I'll come with you."

Petra recalls how she felt that evening. "First, I found it hard to believe that it was possible—eight people in a balloon—I couldn't imagine it. But Günter told me that people had flown in much more primitive contraptions two hundred years ago. He was confident that we could do it too. It really was the only way to avoid the minefields on the border. Later he also explained that it would be impossible for the border guards to shoot down a balloon. It would probably be flying too high, and even if it did get hit, a few holes in the fabric wouldn't be enough to sink it. It would continue to fly—holes and all."

Günter and Peter emphasized that it would be months, maybe even years, until they were ready to go. "That was good news," says Petra. "I realized that the project wasn't nearly as simple as they at first made it out to be. I also remember telling myself over and over not to worry until I was sure that they were really going to carry out their plan."

But Günter and Peter were obsessed with their idea and started work immediately. Using graph paper and long, complicated calculations, they figured out exactly how much fabric they would need for the balloon and what equipment was necessary for the gas-burner. The next step was to find a way to buy what they needed.

"We knew that it would arouse suspicion in Pössneck if we tried to buy that much fabric. The whole thing was damned dangerous."

Günter quit his job at Saalfeld Transport, telling his employers that he was going to take courses to become a truck mechanic. His superiors were understanding and suspected nothing. From that day on, Günter devoted all his time and energy to the balloon project.

"We had figured that we needed almost one thousand square yards of fabric, a huge amount! We drove around to various cities trying to find a store with that much material on hand." They returned from Rudolstadt, Saalfeld, and Jena empty-handed.

Finally, they drove all the way to Gera, capital of Thuringia, in Peter's eighteen-year-old orange Moskwitsch. In the fabric department on the second floor of the large department store on Sorge Street, with clothing, sheets, and towels in the display window, they found what they were looking for—a roll of brown cotton fabric a yard wide, on sale at three marks a yard.

A saleswoman approached them and offered to help the gentlemen.

Peter asked, "Is this material tear resistant?"

"It's not only tear resistant, it's sales resistant as well," she replied. "It's been lying around here for years. That's why the price has been reduced. How much do you need?"

Peter looked around, saw no one nearby, and said, "Eight hundred and eighty yards!"

Peter remembers, "The saleswoman was absolutely stunned and asked what we were going to do with it. I explained that we needed it to line tents for our camping club, adding that we would impregnate the material to waterproof it."

The salesclerk apparently believed Peter's story. She went to the stockroom and returned with good news. "We have enough for you." The two nervous customers paid 2,400 marks in cash which Peter had withdrawn from his savings account.

Then they dragged the heavy rolls of fabric through the store and stuffed them into the boot and onto the back seat of the old Moskwitsch. They waited for nightfall before driving back to Pössneck. Under the protection of darkness, they lugged the rolls across the street and up the steps to the attic bedroom in the Wetzels' house at 22 Tuchmacher Street.

For the next two weeks, the tiny bedroom was hidden under mountains of brown material. Using self-made blueprints as a guide, Günter and Peter spent two full days cutting the material into long triangles and strips. Then Günter sat down in front of their old foot-pedal-operated Gritzner sewing machine with its huge flywheel. "I really had made a few tents in my day, so at least I knew how to operate the machine."

He pushed the ancient machine under one of the slanted attic windows so that the light would fall on the needle and thread. Peter led the material through the machine as Günter sewed the triangles of cloth together. He sometimes worked twelve hours a day without a break until his hands and ankles were swollen and he had tears in his eyes from the strain. Finally, after about two weeks, a pear-shaped balloon emerged from the mess, measuring 50 by 66 feet.

Petra acted as a security guard while the men were working. She set up a large ladder behind the front door and when visitors came she said, "I'm sorry. I can't let you in right now. We're renovating the house and there's a ladder blocking the door." They also installed an auxiliary doorbell in the bedroom so that the man at the sewing machine would be warned in advance if someone wanted to come into the house.

Günter had set up his workshop two storeys below, on the second floor. Rough boards served as workbenches and an old cupboard had been converted to hold various sized hammers, screwdrivers, and saws. A vice was mounted on the unsanded worktable. Günter was particularly proud of his Black & Decker drill, a present from a West German friend. If it had been available at all, such a drill would have cost 350 marks or more in East Germany.

The workshop curtains were drawn to hide the reflection of the welding torch and Peter started to build the gondola and burner system. The noise of drilling was drowned out by news and music broadcasts from the *Voice of East Germany* on an old radio.

First Peter built a collapsible gondola consisting of a steel frame 4 feet 6 inches by 4 feet 6 inches with eight wooden boards forming a floor. He bolted a steel post with holes drilled in it at each corner. He passed a clothesline through the holes to serve as a guardrail around the gondola.

The burner rig that would heat the cold air in the balloon was a great deal more complicated to build than the gondola. It consisted of two bottles of liquid propane, 11.8 inches in diameter, 24.2 pounds in weight, holding 1.45 gallons, which were connected by hoses to a half-inch water pipe with a stopcock, topped by four nozzles leading into a sheet-metal stovepipe that measured 39 inches in length and 5 inches in diameter. The four burner pipes were 5 feet 6 inches long.

Peter built the first burner system within a week. And within two weeks of the first casual mention of building a balloon, their homemade version was ready for testing.

The brown shell was easily portable. When folded, it measured only 3 feet long and 2 feet 6 inches high. The balloon builders, anxious to test their balloon by early April, set out to find an appropriate testing area somewhere south of Pössneck.

In the spring of 1978 the area surrounding the Thuringian Forest was still covered by a thin layer of snow. As usual in April, the weather had been unpredictable and periods of snow and hail were interspersed with periods of sun and rain. They found what seemed to be an ideal place for the test near the little village of Neuenbeuthen, south of the village of Ziegenrück. There lay a large clearing in the woods, surrounded by high pine trees, and accessible only by a narrow sand path. The clearing was well protected from curious eyes.

There was a raised blind for hunters at the edge of the field and Günter spent several evenings there waiting to see if any hunters or townsfolk came around after twilight. Using 8-by-30 binoculars, he studied the area in the moonlight and never saw more than a few rabbits hopping around the clearing. The time had come to test the balloon.

It was April 28, 1978, an hour before midnight. There were few clouds in the sky and the moon shone over the Thuringian countryside. Fifteen miles north of the West German border, about seven miles south of Pössneck, the two men unrolled the long, brown sack on the forest floor. Günter held the neck of the balloon (about three yards in diameter) open and Peter lit the homemade burner with a blowtorch. But the flame was barely three feet long, not long enough to reach the neck of the balloon, which remained as flat as a flounder. They tried for two hours to get the flame high enough to inflate the balloon, but nothing happened.

Grumpy and disappointed, Peter and Günter finally packed their gear and drove home. Günter says, "We were really depressed. We assumed that the problem had to do with our method of inflation and spent the next few days trying to figure out other ways to get hot air into the balloon. We thought that maybe the balloon should be positioned vertically instead of lying flat on the ground, and considered hanging it from a tree. But that was impossible because the balloon was much longer than even the tallest trees in the area."

They spent several weeks looking for a place where the balloon could hang vertically and finally discovered an isolated rock quarry northeast of Pössneck, near Döbritz. Many thousands of years ago, in the Stone Age, people had made their homes in the caves surrounding the quarry, and at weekends the area was crowded with tourists coming to see how their ancestors had lived. During the week, however, it resembled an uninhabited moonscape.

There was a full moon again the night that Peter and Günter lowered their balloon on a rope down the seventy-five-foot quarry wall until it finally hung suspended like an empty sausage skin. Then they drove the Moskwitsch down the steep path leading to the quarry floor, where they lit the burner and held it under the balloon opening. The hot air travelled upward with ease. Just as the balloon seemed to expand slightly, Peter called to Günter in a half-whisper, "God, Günter, there's someone over there! I just saw a head look over the edge of the rocks!"

Peter had indeed seen a shadow in the moonlight, but they would never know if it was a human or an animal. (A few days later they learned that the old quarry was occasionally patrolled at night to guard construction trailers containing valuable equipment.) They quickly packed their tools, tore the balloon from the quarry wall, and stuffed it into the boot of the car. Peter drove away from the quarry without headlights, choosing narrow, unpaved back roads and detours. They had been underway for about ten minutes when they noticed that they were dragging something behind them. The top of the balloon had fallen out of the boot and was already torn in several places.

In a few days the torn balloon was patched and they were ready for new testing grounds. Luck seemed to be against them, however. Something always prevented them from carrying out their tests: either it would start to rain just as they got in the car, or the ground wind was too strong, or there were too many people on the road late at night.

"Near the place where we had first tested the balloon, there was a railroad track running from Lobenstein to Triptis. The train had to cross a bridge spanning a high canyon between Neuenbeuthen and Liebschütz." Peter figured that they could hang the balloon from one of the bridge pillars and stand below the bridge with the blowtorch.

They reconnoitred the area for days, checking the passenger train schedules and observing the freight train traffic late at night. They found that traffic stopped at midnight.

"One night we parked the car a short distance from the bridge and unpacked the balloon. We had to cross a small stream to get to the bridge and, wouldn't you know, there had been a heavy rainstorm the day before, and overnight the stream had turned into a small river. The balloon weighed more than 330 pounds dry, and Günter and I couldn't drag it through the water. Again we had to turn back."

The next time, realizing that they needed all the help they could get, they brought Doris and Petra along. Günter drove ahead and checked out the area from a blind in the forest. Through the high trees he could see the houses in the little village of Neuenbeuthen. The landscape was hilly, covered with dense pinewoods, with occasional oak trees. Günter watched as the last few lights went out at eleven o'clock. Peter arrived with the two women at midnight as arranged.

The two men had invented a new type of launching pad, a kind of pulley with a rope running over a wooden block. Günter climbed the highest tree he could find and attached the pulley to the tip of the tree. Then they used the rope winch to pull the balloon to the top so that it hung diagonally from the tree to the ground. Doris and Petra held the neck of the balloon open while Peter lit the burner. This time the flame, at least nine feet long, shot up to the opening of the balloon. But nothing else happened. The balloon still hung tired and empty from the tree.

Petra says, "I had brought some homemade red currant wine to warm us up. I don't know whether it was the alcohol or the situation, but for some reason, I thought the whole thing was rather funny. In contrast to Günter and Peter who were taking it all very seriously, Doris and I were giddy and silly. The men whispered and cursed and complained because they couldn't inflate the balloon. The fabric fluttered once in a while but that was all."

Günter remembers, "The women giggled like teenagers while we sweated blood and water."

Again they couldn't get the balloon to lift and they were beginning to think that they never would. They were still convinced that the problem was the method of inflation. Refusing to give up, Günter came up with another idea. "We have to build a fan."

And so they built an ingenious blower. It consisted of a large propeller with six sheet metal blades, each about three feet long, powered by a 14 hp, 250 cc MZ motorcycle engine built by Zwickauer Motorworks. The engine turned the propeller at a rate of three thousand rotations per minute and had a capacity of 17,650 cubic feet of air per minute. The engine was equipped with a starter taken from an old motorcycle which they could jump-start from the battery of Peter's Moskwitsch sedan. They found an old Wartburg muffler in a junkyard to cut down the noise of the engine.

Again the balloon builders drove out to the field near Neuenbeuthen with their wives. Again they used the winch to hang the balloon from the high pine trees. They ignited the burner and turned on the fan. The motorcycle engine hummed. Doris and Petra held the balloon open, and Günter directed the stream of cold air from the fan so that it passed over the flame pushing the heated air into the balloon.

The brown cotton cloth fluttered like a fish in shallow water, but the bag would not inflate. Each time they turned off the blowtorch and the fan, the shell deflated completely. Finally, they discovered the cause of the problem. The air was rushing out through the cotton cloth. The material was simply too porous.

Günter and Peter were bitterly disappointed. The women didn't take it quite so seriously. Petra says, "I thought it was funny the way we were rushing around and the way the balloon flapped on the ground." And Doris remembers, "Petra and I were completely out of breath from running up and down the length of the balloon, shaking it so that the hot air could move further up. But we were just wasting our energy."

There was still enough air in the balloon to make it difficult for the four of them to roll it up and pack it into the car. Once again tipsy from the wine that Petra had brought, they squeezed the air out of the balloon like human rolling pins. "We giggled and joked like goblins in the forest," says Petra smiling. "If anyone had seen us, they would have thought that we had just escaped from the nearest insane asylum."

It took several days to cut the balloon into tiny pieces and meticulously burn it piece by piece in the large coal furnace in the Strelzyks' cellar. Peter and Günter had learned about building balloons the hard way. They sat and watched as 2,400 marks' worth of material literally went up in smoke. Tired and disappointed, but not ready to give up, they immediately started planning their next move.

7

Second
Thoughts

Another month had passed. The crocuses in the Strelzyks' garden had come and gone. The trees in the Pössneck marketplace were in full bloom. As always on Labour Day in East Germany, May 1, the Blue Shirt members of the Free German Youth marched through the streets of the town waving red flags. The Young Pioneers and old Party veterans marched in brigades with their factory groups. Banners proclaimed:

> "Our May Day pledge: Freedom and Peace Forever!"
> "German Democratic Republic: true land of the people."
> "Strive to Fulfil Socialist Objectives!"

Other banners depicting Lenin, Brezhnev, and Honecker were carried through the streets throughout East Germany.

The Strelzyks and Wetzels stood with other spectators and watched the parade in Pössneck, as Frank and Andreas Strelzyk marched by with the Young Pioneers. When Peter saw the hundreds of banners and flags fluttering in the wind, he thought to himself, "Damn, wouldn't they be perfect for our new balloon!"

Peter and Günter were in agreement. They would start immediately on another balloon. Between the two of them, they had enough money in their savings accounts to buy the material they needed.

Günter says, "I was in a hurry because I was, in fact, illegally unemployed. Eventually someone from the State Security Service would wonder what I had been doing with my time since quitting my job. They are suspicious of anyone who disappears or stays away from work for too long."

In the first week of May, they started over from the very beginning. "With practice and experience behind us this time, we thought it would be much easier. All we needed was a new shell. And we had learned from our mistake. Now we knew that we needed a better quality fabric, something that was airtight." So they designed a three-part test to determine which material would be most suitable for their next balloon. They would use the method to test carefully various types of fabric for heat and air resistance.

They bought samples of four different textiles from a fabric store in Pössneck: umbrella silk, nylon jacket-liner, and two grades of synthetic taffeta. The system they devised to test the density of the fabric was simple. They drilled a quarter-inch hole in the side of a plastic vacuum cleaner hose and inserted a U-shaped glass tube into it so that it was airtight. They marked the tube at intervals and filled it half way with water. When the vacuum cleaner was turned on and the end of the hose was left open, nothing happened to the water. But when the end of the hose was covered with fabric, the water in the tube was sucked up to one of the marks on the glass. The experiment was carried out with each of the four samples. They stretched the fabric over the end of the hose and read on their scale which fabric offered the greatest resistance.

Testing for hot-air permeability was also a simple procedure. "We put a candle in a deep pot and stretched the four samples over the pot one after the other. All we had to do was hold our hands over the pot to determine which fabric allowed hot air to escape."

To determine heat resistance they put the samples next to

each other in the kitchen oven and increased the temperature until the material started to burn or fall apart. "The best piece of cloth started to catch fire at five hundred degrees Fahrenheit."

They found that the umbrella fabric would best serve their purpose, but at seven marks a yard, it was also the most expensive. They settled for the heavy taffeta which was almost as good and cost only 5.30 marks a yard, a difference of more than 1,500 marks.

To save time, they wanted to buy all the material in one place if possible. Afraid of being questioned in Pössneck, they drove one hundred miles to East Germany's second-largest city, Leipzig. They pretended that the Gera Sailing Club had sent them to the department store. When the salesgirl heard that they wanted to buy 880 yards of fabric, she called her supervisor. He made a telephone call, turned to Peter and said, "We can have the material ready for you by tomorrow."

Peter and Günter almost panicked. "We seriously debated whether it was wise to come back the next day, and we half expected to be stopped by the People's Police for questioning before we got out of the store." They overcame their fear, however, and returned the following day. The material was packed and waiting for them—880 yards of multi-coloured taffeta for 4,800 marks. They paid part of the bill in cash, but had to write a cheque for the rest.

"I had a terrible feeling when I wrote out the cheque," says Peter. "Not only did this give them a record of the transaction, but I had to show identification with my address on it. And I didn't live in Gera."

Taking advantage of the fact that they were already in Leipzig, they bought a motor for the old sewing machine. They were both impatient this time and the cheap Czechoslovakian motor for 140 marks would speed things up considerably.

Again the curtains were drawn at the Wetzels' house. They set up ladders and paint buckets in and around the house to discourage visitors. Günter sat at the newly motorized sewing machine while Doris, Peter, and Petra took turns leading the precut fabric across the sewing table. They used the same pattern they had used before because there seemed to be no reason to alter the size of the balloon. They progressed quickly and this time the balloon was finished in a little over a week.

The lines connecting the balloon to the gondola were sewn on and this time they added a valve to release hot air. They had learned about the necessity of the valve by chance when they were halfway through the project. Taking a television break one evening, the Strelzyks had happened to see a West German television show with neighbours.

"The series was called *Highway to Adventure*. I wasn't paying much attention to the screen until suddenly there was talk about ballooning. Of course, Doris and I were fascinated, and our neighbours seemed to find it interesting too. The film even showed a balloon in flight. The narrator explained that a rubber valve had been built into the top of the balloon to facilitate landing. When the flap was opened, hot air escaped through the hole and the balloon sank.

"Later, we built a valve far up at the top of our balloon similar to the one in the film. We sewed in a real hinge which was attached to a metal ring covered with fabric and sewn together. We then attached a long line from the gondola with which we could open and close the valve. Under normal conditions, the hot air pushing the valve against the wall of the balloon would keep the valve closed, and it would only open when the line was pulled."

The balloon in the movie was 1,300 cubic yards. Doris was so involved in the film that she almost let their secret slip. Forgetting that their neighbours were in the room, she proudly blurted out, "Ours is twice as big as that one!" Peter turned white and looked at his wife imploringly as he poured himself a large glass of schnapps. But fortunately the guests had been engrossed in the show and hadn't heard Doris' comment.

It was now the end of May 1978. The second balloon was completed. The gondola had been improved upon and no longer had such a shaky wooden floor. Instead, they had replaced it with thin but sturdy steel plates, set between iron braces. The tin was only .03 inch thick and was covered with green plastic. Peter had welded diagonal iron struts underneath the steel to stabilize it. They tested it and found that it easily held their weight.

After a lot of searching, Peter finally found a small trailer for only 450 marks at the People's Owned Exchange for Machines and Surplus Material in Gera, a State-run enterprise selling motor vehicles and accessories. It had two axles and was exactly the same size as the gondola, 1.5 by 1.5 yards. Peter welded the trailer coupling to his Moskwitsch and designed the gondola to fit right on top of the trailer. With four iron stays in the corners and the hand ropes running through the stays, it looked like any other trailer on the road. They folded the balloon, packed it on top of the gondola, and covered the whole thing with a tarpaulin.

"If we had been stopped by the police, we would have said that we were on our way to a camping trip and they probably would have believed us." At last they were ready to test the new balloon.

It was a warm day toward the end of May. But it was still rather cool toward evening and dampness settled in on the ground. This time it was Peter's turn to man the hunter's blind in the woods near Neuenbeuthen, so he left at eight o'clock in the Moskwitsch and was followed three hours later by Günter, Doris, and Petra with the "camping equipment".

By now, setting up the apparatus was a routine matter for the two couples. First they assembled the cold-air blower and then put the gondola on the ground, attaching the lines of the balloon to the corner braces of the gondola so that there were three lines attached to each corner. Then they rolled the multicoloured balloon out on the ground of the clearing and unpacked a new piece of equipment—a home-built blowtorch.

Finally, they were ready to begin. They started the motor. In spite of the built-in muffler, a deafening roar shattered the stillness of the night as air was sucked into the neck of the balloon by the powerful propeller. "We had expected it to be loud but were hoping, since the main road was less than a mile away, that the noise of a motorcycle wouldn't seem unusual."

Günter and the two women had to steady themselves on the ground and hold on tightly to the circular neck of the balloon to counterbalance the pressure of the air. Peter ignited the blowtorch and the burner. The flame was higher than it had been—about twelve to twenty feet—because the gas was now streaming from four large propane bottles instead of only two as with the first balloon.

"The flame was forced back for the first few seconds, our wives had to jump sideward to avoid it, and I singed my hair. But then the updraft was so strong that it took all my strength to hold on to the burner." Peter was pleased with the flame.

Success on the first try! Within five minutes the huge green, blue, and beige striped sack slowly started to lift. The top half swayed upward, making a slapping sound as it filled with air. The bottom half expanded, stiffened, and lifted from the wet ground. And then the pear-shaped hot-air balloon towered over the clearing.

"This time the air stayed inside, right where we wanted it," says Peter proudly.

Günter beams when he talks about it today. "The first time you see a balloon that size, it's fantastic! Especially if you built it yourself!"

The two women retreated to the edge of the clearing to get a proper view of the scene. "Standing too close to it, we were blinded by the light of the burner flame. But from a short distance away, it was simply a beautiful sight . . . strange . . . fantastic . . . dreamlike. There it was. The stars in the sky, the dark woods, the field, and our wonderful balloon right there in the middle, like an overgrown mushroom. We stood at the edge of the woods with our mouths open in astonishment."

Petra suggested, "Let's leave it there until it gets a little lighter so that we can really see it."

The others laughed, and Peter said, "I think it would be a lot smarter to get the hell away from here before dawn."

The balloon hung there inflated for fifteen or twenty minutes with the burner in the gondola and the flame reaching upward toward the centre of the balloon. It seemed perfect until Peter, the realistic "activist", put a damper on the cheerful mood of his companions. He tested the lines connecting the gondola to the balloon and found that he was able to pull the side of the mammoth balloon down with one hand. Disappointed, he yelled, "Damn it! The thing is inflated but it has no lifting power. It's not strong enough to lift us or anything else."

They discussed the matter. They tried to turn the burner flame higher. They shook the propane bottles. But nothing helped. The flame remained low. Finally Peter admitted that the air in the balloon simply wasn't hot enough to propel the balloon with eight people in it.

But the balloon was off the ground. They had come a long way since the initial test with the first balloon. Doris unpacked four glasses from a plastic bag, filled them with currant wine, and the four tired friends drank to their partial success.

"Bon voyage!" someone said.

"Here's to a new life in the West!"

"Westward ho!"

"Prost!"

Günter sighed. "I still couldn't believe that we had built this giant in our tiny bedroom."

They closed the burner vents and the flames died down. Günter tugged at the line leading to the ventilation flap of the balloon. The hot air escaped through the opening and the balloon slowly shrivelled up. They packed the balloon, the gondola, and the propane bottles under the tarpaulin in the trailer, and drove the short distance on the narrow sand road until they reached the main road that runs via Neuenbeuthen to Altenbeuthen, then in the direction of Ziegenrück.

They were discussing possible solutions to the problem of increasing the dynamic lift of the balloon when suddenly, as if from nowhere, a huge metal vehicle loomed ahead of them on the opposite side of the road. It had no headlights and was moving very slowly toward them.

Peter says, "I didn't even actually see it until I had almost passed it. But when I did, it really gave me a jolt! It was a People's Army panzer. Behind the tank there was a column of smaller military vehicles and foot soldiers marching in a goose step fashion on the side of the road." Günter shouted at Peter to drive faster. But Peter continued at the same speed.

They finally reached the end of the convoy, but they didn't feel safe until they were back in Pössneck. "I couldn't stop thinking about how lucky we had been," says Peter. "I kept imagining what would have happened if they had arrived thirty minutes earlier and discovered us in the clearing with the inflated balloon."

Günter adds, "It must have been a night manoeuvre of the National People's Army. There were probably soldiers creeping around all over the woods. I suddenly realized for the first time what a dangerous game we were playing. All four of us would have spent several years behind bars if they had caught us."

Throughout the month of June, the two men worked on the burner trying to devise a way to increase the length of the flame, which they figured would have to be at least thirty feet long to heat the air sufficiently. "We needed three to five times more pressure than we had had at Neuenbeuthen if the balloon were to carry all eight of us."

They enlarged the burner vent again. They tried different types of fuel, including gasoline, propane, and even a mixture of the two. "There was no sense using gasoline, though. The flame flared up, but it was nowhere near as high as the propane flame. And we would have needed too much gasoline for a thirty-minute flight. It would have been too heavy to carry."

It seemed that the more difficult the problem was, the more determined the two men were to solve it. During the day they continued to take on electrical jobs. They spent evenings and nights in the workshop at Günter's place or driving to out-of-the-way places around Pössneck to test their burner. They had become much more careful since the near brush in the middle of the night with the soldiers, who had apparently come from the People's Army barracks near Wurzbach, a few miles from the border.

Meanwhile Frank, the Strelzyks' fourteen-year-old son, had begun to suspect that something was going on. He wondered why his parents had started going out so often.

"Mother kept telling me that they had been invited by people from work, or that they were going to visit the Wetzels, or to the movies. Then she would tell me that she had a meeting at work or a Party meeting. Somehow it all seemed a bit strange to me because my parents, especially my father, had never enjoyed going out all the time. They were always happy to sit in front of the television set with me."

Frank, a bright child, almost precocious for his age, takes after his father and is interested in anything mechanical. His voice had just broken then, and he had shot up to five feet seven inches. He was letting his black hair grow longer and combed it in casual-looking waves across his forehead. Like his classmates, he was wild about rock music. "I used to listen to all the pop and rock programmes on radio station Bavaria III." Elvis Presley was his favourite, but he was also a fan of The Puhdys, an East German rock band known in both parts of Germany for its good lyrics.

Frank was in class 7A at the Ernst Thälmann School and, like the rest of his friends, was active in the Free German Youth. "We went camping, had scavenger hunts, and did a lot of fun things. I wasn't so crazy about the political part though. All they did was repeat the same junk over and over again."

Doris and Peter had purposely kept the balloon a secret from their son. "We wanted to spare him the burden of it, and anyway, we weren't all that sure that anything would ever come of it. We also thought that it would be very difficult for a child that age to keep it secret. After all, a giant hot-air balloon was a pretty exciting thing for a young boy. It's the kind of thing kids like to impress their friends with. The most casual remark would have endangered the whole project, not to mention our safety."

But Frank wasn't as gullible as they thought. "I wandered into the garage one day when my father and Günter were building something and I saw what looked like an aircraft propeller. My father acted kind of strange when he saw me there and told me to come in and close the door behind me. I got a closer look at the propeller and asked my father what it was."

Frank's father exchanged a look with Günter and finally answered, "It's a sort of blower that the Agricultural Production Enterprise uses to dry hay. It's not working right, and they asked us to try to fix it."

Frank didn't buy the story. "It didn't make sense, because my father had never had anything to do with the APE before. After a while I forgot about it though."

When he went into the garage a week or two later, the propeller had disappeared. Now there was a giant roll of fabric in the corner. His father came into the garage shortly after he did and told him that it was a large tent. Again, Frank tells us, he thought something was strange, because in the past his father had always explained everything to him in detail and he hadn't bothered to mention the tent to him.

Peter felt uneasy about lying to Frank and decided to share the secret with his son. "Frank is such a sensible boy and I thought that it would probably be safer to trust him with the secret project than leave him guessing."

The opportunity to tell Frank presented itself one evening when they were all sitting in the living room watching television. A news item came on about a recent border incident between the Soviet Union and the People's Republic of China. This led to a discussion.

Today Frank remembers what they said. "We talked about how there would probably be a war some day between Red China and Russia. If so, our militia, the National People's Army, would most certainly be called on to help our Soviet brothers."

Peter said, "That will probably all happen just at the time when you're in the service and then you'll have to march with them to risk your life fighting the Chinese."

"I'm not crazy about the idea myself," said Frank. "But I don't have much choice about getting drafted. If I happen to be in the service then, I won't have much to say about fighting the Chinese either."

Peter answered that he knew what they could do to prevent all this from happening. "We can leave East Germany and go to live somewhere else—a country that isn't a member of the Warsaw Pact. Then maybe . . ."

"Yeah, sure," interrupted Frank. "But how do you expect to get out of East Germany? Fly?"

His father paused before answering, choosing his words carefully. "Maybe. If there were an aeroplane waiting to take you and Mother and Andreas to West Germany, would you want to go?"

Frank nodded. "Sure, why not? As long as we all went together. . . . I hear it's a lot nicer over there anyway. But what's the sense of talking about it when we don't have an aeroplane?"

Peter studied his son's face for a long time. "Well, you're right. We don't have an aeroplane. But we do have something similar. . . ."

Finally Peter and Frank went to the garage. "There it was. A giant balloon! Father showed it to me and told me the whole story from beginning to end. He explained why he and Günter wanted to go to West Germany, told me all about the first balloon, and the test with the new balloon. He said that we were almost ready to go."

The Wetzels had also spent the last several days discussing the flight and the balloon. Petra had lost her nerve.

"I didn't know what to expect in the West. I had heard that things weren't quite as golden there as they appeared on television. And Günter and I had built a nice life in East Germany. The house was finally livable and I was proud of it. I liked my job. What more could we want? On the other hand, I still remembered the Berlin Wall, the barbed wire, the mined belt. I knew that I would never have the opportunity to travel to foreign countries if I stayed in East Germany. The lack of freedom bothered me, but I had no proof that a democracy was any better. Basically, I was scared to death. The balloon was beautiful to look at, but I doubted that it could safely carry eight people across the border."

For several days, Günter relentlessly defended the plan. "I wanted out of East Germany. I had made up my mind and I wanted to leave as quickly as possible. I felt that every day I spent in East Germany was wasted."

But after days of argument and discussion, he too began to have second thoughts. "We still hadn't found a burner system that worked. I couldn't see how we would get the balloon's air hot enough to carry the weight of eight people. I calculated that, at best, the balloon could carry half of the necessary 1,700 pounds. I finally decided to speak to Peter. I told him that I had lost faith in the project, that I no longer believed the flight was plausible. I also told him about Petra's fear of crashing and that we wanted to back out."

Peter was understanding. "I wasn't angry with Günter. It was his choice. Of course, I took it hard at first. But I could understand why he felt the way he did." Peter also realized that with the passenger weight cut in half, the chance of success would double.

The two friends decided to sever their relationship entirely until Peter was either in the West, or had given up his plan. "We didn't want to risk involving Petra and Günter as accomplices." Peter and Günter brought everything that might connect Günter with the balloon to Peter's house on Altenburg Circle.

They found it difficult to shake hands for the last time. "We searched for the right words to say and just stood there looking at each other. We had already been through so much together." Günter, always taciturn, finally said, "Good luck." Then he walked away.

8

===

A
Double
Life

The Strelzyks continued to work on the project alone. Peter, determined to find a solution to the burner problem, spent all his spare time in the laundry room experimenting. He tried a larger valve and then a smaller one. He shortened the burner pipe and then lengthened it again. He tried different mixtures of gases. Nothing seemed to work. At night he drove to the woods south of Pössneck and tested the burner, with varying results.

"Sometimes the flame was larger than it had been in previous experiments and sometimes it was smaller. I was never satisfied with it. But I was getting impatient and made up my mind to attempt a flight in August."

The Strelzyks told neighbours, friends, and colleagues that they were taking a short holiday. They stacked the balloon, gondola, propane bottles, blowtorch, and everything else they thought they might need on the trailer, covered it with the tarpaulin, and drove off.

For nine days they crisscrossed the southeastern foothills of the Thuringian Forest in the car. They drove to Lake Hohenwartestal and the Bleiloch reservoir—only a mile from the Berlin Autobahn and two and a half miles from the border. They slept in a tent or, when the ground was wet, on the reclining seats of the car. Three or four times along the way, they practised setting up the balloon. Frank took over Günter's job of holding the neck of the balloon open and starting the cold air blower. Twice the balloon lifted from the ground but never with enough tractive force to carry the family.

"We finally gave up and drove back to Pössneck." The only positive result of the holiday was that they had found an ideal point of departure. It was a clearing in the woods, one mile west of the highway from Pössneck to Lobenstein, between the villages of Oberlemnitz and Heinersdorf. "There was a small pine grove above a little railroad track from Lobenstein to Saalfeld. And in the middle was this completely isolated area. We made a mental note of the place."

They returned to Pössneck to find the town in an uproar. There had been an escape and the whole town was talking about it.

Günter Wetzel was there when it happened and he re-members the incident clearly: "There was only one topic of conversation last August. Everyone had heard on West German television that three people had escaped from Pöss-neck to Kassel in a low-flying fertilizer plane. The most prominent of the refugees was thirty-eight-year-old Doctor Johannes Pfützenreuther, Head of Male Surgery at the Pöss-neck Policlinic. I knew him personally because he had oper-ated on me for appendicitis."

Peter, who had returned from his trip discouraged and disheartened, found the news of the doctor's escape heart-warming. "If they can do it, so can we! Even without an aeroplane." His only concern was that the air over East Ger-many would be more closely monitored than ever before.

Dr. Pfützenreuther had escaped with a friend, twenty-seven-year-old Georg Brommer, a machinist, and Rainer Weiland, also twenty-seven years old, an agricultural pilot. They had made their escape in an old single-engine Czech-built plane, a Let Z-37A Cmelak, flying only 650 feet above the ground. The pilot landed the plane safely on a ploughed field outside Kassel.

The citizens of Pössneck were amazed. They stood in small groups in the street and talked about nothing but the young doctor's thrilling escape. Peter identified with the doctor when he heard him quoted on West German television. He had left East Germany "because of the blatant contrast between the reality of daily life in East Germany and claims of the Party propaganda machine. Life had become unbearable."

With renewed enthusiasm, Peter continued his experiments. One night in the autumn of 1978 he seriously burned himself while testing the burner. "The back of my hand was one painful blister." The next day he told the doctor that he had burned himself welding, an occupational hazard.

Frank helped his father whenever possible. Peter says, "I had to make sure that Frank kept up in school. I didn't want his life to change yet. But he was very involved in our project. The balloon was the only thing he cared about. He was always volunteering to drill holes and tighten screws. I reminded him of the consequences if the hoses weren't properly attached—our lives could depend on it. I double-checked everything he did. But I could have saved myself the trouble, for everything he did was one hundred percent perfect."

It was a damp, rainy autumn. In Thuringia and elsewhere in Germany snow fell early, forcing the Strelyzks to call a halt to their nightly tests. But Peter and Frank continued to experiment in the cellar. They wanted to have everything ready to go by the following spring when weather conditions improved.

The Strelzyks led a double life. On the surface, everything seemed the same as it had always been. Peter ran his installation business alone now because Günter had left and found a job as a truck driver. Doris continued to work at the Pössneck Savings Bank and the children were enrolled at the Ernst Thälmann School. Both children knew, of course, that they were never to mention the balloon.

"We tried several times to trick Andreas into mentioning

the project, but he proved as tight-lipped as an old man."
Andreas (or "Fitscher" as he was called because he was so
active) continued to attend his Young Pioneer meetings
once a week.

The aim of this branch of the Socialist Unity Party, to
which ninety-nine percent of six- to thirteen-year-old East
German children officially belong, is to "cooperate with parents and schools in an effort to raise class-conscious young
Socialists." Ten-year-old Andreas wore the red uniform scarf
and proudly sang the "Battle Song of the Thälmann Pioneers" at Party functions and celebrations:

> Industrious and hearty,
> We're the youngest fighting party,
> Happy and proud of our home
> And the woods and fields we roam.
> We offer our hands in friendship
> To other children of the world
> And proudly carry the banner
> Of the Republic we adore. . . .

Frank, at fourteen, had already outgrown the Pioneers
and was member number 9021643 of the Free German
Youth. "Each time I met with my FGY comrades I thought,
'If only they knew that we have a balloon at home. . . .' "

And alone, he continually reminded himself that if he
made a mistake and mentioned the balloon, his whole family
could end up in prison. Each time he made a date to play
soccer with his friends, he secretly wondered if he would
still be around for the game.

Christmas came and they were still there. Peter says,
"Since I was convinced that this would be our last Christmas
in Pössneck, I tried to make it a special one for my family. I
chopped down a six-foot-tall pine tree from the forest and
Doris decorated it with bright balls and tinsel. We had potato salad with bratwurst, and chocolates for dessert."

Knowing that they would have to leave everything behind, Peter and Doris decided not to give each other presents that year. "But we wanted the children to have a nice
Christmas. Frank got a very valuable present, a Bulgarian-

built Grundig MK-27 cassette recorder costing more than six hundred marks. Andreas received several battery-powered cars and some books."

But Frank had prepared the most original Christmas presents of all. He had seen a West German science-fiction series featuring a space ship called *Andromeda*. He spent hours in his room with the door closed sewing the word *Andromeda* on his parents' and little brother's windcheaters. Each member of the family was given a rank: his father was Commander, mother was Copilot, Frank himself was Navigator, and Andreas was assigned the rank of Steward. Peter and Doris were pleased with the surprise, but later, for security reasons, they had to remove the lettering from all the jackets.

The snow on the ground didn't melt until April that year. It wasn't until then that the Strelzyks could resume their outdoor tests. They still hadn't figured out how to increase the burner flame enough to heat the air in the balloon sufficiently.

Peter burned up enormous amounts of gas in his tests and every two weeks he took the empty propane bottles to the Pössneck filling station to refill them. He told the attendant there that he was not using all the gas himself, but that some of it was for a few older people in the neighbourhood who couldn't get there themselves.

Toward the end of May, Peter stumbled on the solution to the problem that had plagued him for so long. "I turned a half-empty propane bottle upside down in the yard to empty it and it slipped out of my hands. Suddenly propane shot out of the bottle with tremendous pressure through the open tap and the whole yard was in fog. If someone had lit a match, the whole area would have gone up in flames."

Then it dawned on him that it was really very easy to increase the pressure. All he had to do was install the bottles upside down. That same night he tested his theory in the woods. On ignition, a forty-foot flame shot out of the stovepipe. The propane was now released in liquid form and directly hit the flame.

Exactly one year and four months after the idea was first conceived, the homemade balloon was ready and the Strelzyks had only to wait for favourable wind and weather conditions.

"Of course, we were all terribly excited, but we tried to hide our impatience. The last thing we wanted now was to draw attention to ourselves. It would have ruined everything."

So the Strelzyks felt compelled to participate in yet another Socialist celebration. On May 27 throughout East Germany there are several thousand simultaneous initiation ceremonies in which young people pledge to dedicate their lives to Socialist principles. This year it was Frank's turn to be initiated with several hundred other children aged fourteen and fifteen at the municipal Civic Centre. Doris and Peter sat in the audience with the other parents.

Frank Strelzyk was probably the only one of the 270,516 youths to be initiated that day in 1979 who knew that his "Acceptance to the Community of Socialist Workers" was also his farewell to the German Democratic Republic.

The stage was decorated with flowers and flags. Members of the Free German Youths, in blue shirts and jeans, formed an honour guard. The candidates marched into the room properly dressed for the ceremony, girls in skirts and blouses and boys in suits and ties. The regional orchestra played the anthem as the audience sang along: "Rebuilt from ruin. . . ."

The Master of Ceremonies from the Pössneck Party Headquarters began: "You can now look forward to a happy and fruitful life at the side of millions of workers in our Socialist fatherland. You live in a revolutionary period, a period of transition from Capitalism to Socialism. Devote yourselves to peace and progress for mankind and the Party of the working class. You are truly the children of Socialism and it is up to you to defend and hold on to the achievements of the last thirty years."

The boys and girls approached the stage in groups. The master of ceremonies recited a pledge. Four times he asked, "Are you prepared to continue to learn about Socialism and respect it, to work and fight to protect it against every imperialist attack?" Four times the boys and girls answered, "Yes, we promise."

Frank says that he did not actually repeat the text. He just moved his lips.

Relatives and friends attended a very pleasant party that afternoon in the Strelzyks' backyard. Peter had set up tables and chairs and Doris had prepared a buffet of cold cuts. Frank was allowed to drink as well when his future was toasted. "It was a really nice farewell party," he said later.

Over the next few days, Peter once again checked out the area between Heinersdorf and Oberlemnitz. Everything was ready. There was only one problem. They were completely dependent on the weather and, unfortunately, there was an unusually long rainy period in May. "Rain was the one thing we didn't need," says Peter. "It would weigh down the balloon."

The weather started to improve toward the end of June, and the first of July was as warm and sunny as it is supposed to be in summer. Day after day, the Strelzyks followed the weather forecasts on East and West German stations. They were particularly interested in the sailing forecasts on radio station Bavaria III, which gave detailed reports of wind direction and speed.

Frank had developed his own method of determining weather and wind conditions while he was at school. On the morning of Tuesday, July 3, 1979, he arrived punctually at 7 A.M. in the classroom and sat at his desk. Through the window he could see the roofs of the town. He had only five hours of classes that day—mathematics, biology, chemistry, geography, and mathematics again.

"The first hour we went through rational numbers, equations, fractions, and other stuff. But I wasn't paying much attention to what was going on. I spent the whole hour looking out the window at the Karl Marx Publishing House. I would deliberately drop a ruler or pencil on the floor and bend down to pick it up. From under my desk I could look out the window and see the weather vane on the City Hall."

Just as his teacher, Mrs. Drechsler, was discussing prime numbers, Frank saw that the weather vane was pointing in a southerly direction. The wind was steady from the north— just the right direction for their flight.

During the biology lesson, when the rest of the class was learning about plant reproduction, Frank observed that the wind direction was holding. In the third lesson, the chemistry teacher, Mr. Wunsch, carried out an experiment for the class. "He poured sulphur from a little bottle into a test tube and heated the tube over a Bunsen burner flame. Then he added oxygen and the sulphur disappeared, leaving sodium oxide." Frank dropped his pencil again and saw that, although the wind was still coming from the north, there were now clouds gathering in the sky.

Instead of geography, they had an unexpected lesson in physics with Mr. Linke. "I couldn't believe that he was working with propane gas that morning. He was trying to show changes that take place in gases, that the volume increases under pressure and decreases when cooled. I knew that our balloon worked the same way."

Throughout the afternoon lesson with Mrs. Drechsler, the weather vane was still facing the right direction and the sky was blue and cloudless again. "The teacher called on me when I was peering out the window from under my desk, and I had no idea what the question had been. I stuttered and acted as if I had been passing something to my neighbour. Mrs. Drechsler reprimanded me for being so inattentive."

School was over at a quarter to twelve. Frank shoved his bookcase under his arm and left the building quickly. Once outside, he looked up again and saw a few wispy clouds drifting across the sky. He crossed the railroad tracks at Frieden Street just as the train from Saalfeld had to stop at the crossing. "I watched the smoke from the train and saw that it was being carried in the direction that we wanted the wind to carry us. I knew that if nothing changed, we would leave that night."

And nothing changed. Frank returned home to find his father standing on the balcony looking up at the sky. "Well, kid, start packing!"

Doris had had a hectic day at the Pössneck Savings Bank. "It was just one of those days. The bank was full of customers from early in the morning until closing time. I had to open a lot of new accounts and close several, which involved calculating interest, processing new accounts, and so on." As usual she ate in the little canteen and paid with an employee coupon that had cost her 2.75 marks. On the way to the canteen she, too, looked out the window and noticed that the weather looked favourable.

Early in the afternoon Doris had to attend a course about bank fraud. She arrived home at about three-thirty, and young Frank greeted her at the door. "Mom, I hope you're not as tired as you look. We're going to leave tonight!"

Andreas came home exhausted from two hours of sports that afternoon. He had done his homework after school and gone to play soccer with a friend. Later he watched television and saw a report on the *Skylab*. "I hoped that the *Skylab* wouldn't crash down that night. It might hit our balloon! I was pretty tired by ten o'clock."

Peter and Frank drove to the filling station to fill the propane bottles and were told that there was a supply shortage. "I really cursed," says Peter. "We had to drive all the way to Eversdorf, thirteen miles, where the metal factory had a filling station. There we were able to fill seven bottles at 8.50 apiece."

That afternoon the two adults drank coffee together and made final plans. Doris, getting more and more nervous as the day wore on, took two tranquillizers. In the evening she made a rich bean soup with bacon and they watched the show *Between Meals* starring Gisela Schlüter on West German television.

Doris and Peter collected their identification and social security papers. "If the bureaucrats in West Germany are anything like those in the East, we'll need everything," thought Doris.

Just before it was time to leave, she cleaned the house, washed the dishes, and even put clean sheets on the bed. Peter laughed at her and said, "Don't be ridiculous. We're not coming back anyway." The German housewife in Doris answered, "I don't want them to think that we were a messy family when they search the house later. . . ."

Before they left, the Strelzyks peeked through their curtains watching the lights go out in neighbouring houses until the last light in the retired mayor's house across the street was out. As they locked the door behind them at ten-thirty, the only lights to be seen were in the Police Station windows on the corner. They went through the house directly to the garage so that the neighbours wouldn't see them leaving.

Doris was the last one out of the house. She waited for the children to leave before making secret arrangements for their pet cat, Purzel. "Fortunately, the children were too excited to think about what might happen to the cat. I felt guilty about abandoning him but I told myself that cats know how to survive. I was sure that someone would find him and give him a home."

She placed a stool under the half-opened window in the kitchen so that the cat could get in and out at will. Then she left the house. She had dressed warmly like her husband, who was wearing a heavy yellow jacket. "We didn't want to be too warm because we knew that the flames would be hot. On the other hand, it would be cold at five to six thousand feet, and we would be up there for at least thirty minutes."

Peter packed a small imitation-leather suitcase in the trunk. In it were tools, photographs, and a few personal belongings. He instructed the boys to lie down on the seat so that no one would see that they were out so late.

Andreas sat next to his brother on the back seat of the Moskwitsch, Peter took the wheel, and Doris sat beside him in the passenger seat as they drove out of town pulling the trailer behind them. Peter nervously smoked one cigarette after another.

Eleven-year-old Andreas remembers: "Just before we left, Mommy said that we were going away that night. She didn't say where we were going though, only that it was very important that I should do everything she told me. Then she helped me get dressed. I had to wear long underwear, a heavy sweater, my parka with the hood, and heavy shoes. I didn't notice that the trailer was behind us until we were driving down the street. Then I figured that we had brought the balloon with us, too, and guessed that we were going somewhere to blow it up again as we had done on holiday. But when I started to ask Mommy about it, she put her finger to her lips and told me to be quiet. Then I fell asleep."

Frank was too excited to sleep. He sat there with his own little brown leather suitcase, similar to his father's, on his lap. In it he had packed tools, flashlights, and a first-aid kit. It was held together with a wide brown leather band. "I was really glad that we were finally leaving. But I was very nervous too," admits Frank. "I was afraid that we might get caught before we managed to blow up the balloon."

Doris and Frank had similar thoughts as they drove along in the Moskwitsch. "We talked about it later. We both felt a strange combination of fear and excitement in our stomachs. There was so much that could go wrong. We might get caught before we even took off."

Doris stared ahead through the darkness and remembered a dream she had had several times lately. "The four of us were in the gondola and it rose in the air. Then suddenly everything started going around in circles. One after another we all fell out of the gondola. Before I hit the ground, I would awake covered with sweat."

9

East
or
West?

Peter drove the car past the police station down Oberlinder Street to Ranis, a suburb of Pössneck, then onto the main road bypassing Ziegenrück and Liebschütz. The streets were nearly empty and they only passed two cars on the whole trip. Near Unterlemnitz he turned right onto a narrow road. "I drove about nine hundred yards, turned the engine off, and drifted down a little slope to the edge of the woods and the clearing. The car was hidden under the trees so that it was hardly visible."

They sat in the car for thirty minutes. Andreas slept and the other three hardly said a word. Doris opened a thermos bottle and they sipped hot coffee for warmth. Finally Peter said, "I think it's safe. Let's get started." As they got out of the car, Peter put his arm around his wife and son and said, "No matter what happens, we'll all be together." Frank answered, "Don't worry, Pop. I have a feeling we're going to make it."

They lifted the gondola from the trailer, loosening the corner screws so that it could be set up and inflated quickly. They assembled it and secured it to the ground in the clearing with long iron rings.

"Then we set up the cold air blower and got the blowtorch

ready. We loaded everything we needed—flashlights, matches, butane bottles to ignite the burner, altimeter—into the gondola. Finally we opened the flap covering the trailer, lifted the balloon out, and unrolled it on the ground. We stretched the neck of the balloon over the blower and secured it with a line. Within minutes we were ready to start the motorcycle engine, which sounded terribly loud to us."

The balloon gradually filled with air. Peter looked up at the sky with concern as the stars slowly disappeared behind clouds. He rationalized: "A few clouds won't hurt us as long as we're careful to stay below them."

Three or four minutes later the balloon was already half full of cold air. Frank and Doris removed the cold air blower and Peter ignited the blowtorch and held the fifteen-foot-long flame to the neck of the balloon. Then he ordered Frank to assemble the burner. He quickly attached the stovepipe and tightened it. On his father's command, he lit it.

For fifteen or twenty seconds, the combined heat of the burner and blowtorch warmed the air in the balloon, causing a powerful dynamic lift that pushed the balloon upward. The lines connecting the balloon to the gondola were stretched nearly to breaking point. Peter was momentarily blinded by the glow of the two flames. His wife watched from a distance as the balloon filled and hovered over the clearing. "I checked to make sure that all the seams were holding together. Everything was fine."

It had taken less than ten minutes to inflate the balloon. Peter yelled, "Come on! Quickly! Let's go!" He extinguished the blowtorch and threw it to the ground. Frank climbed over the guardrail between the corner braces while Doris ran to the parked car to get Andreas.

He had been watching the activity in the clearing with half-opened eyes and saw for the first time how large the balloon was. He remembers: "I was sort of half asleep in the car and woke up when I heard the motorcycle engine. Daddy and Frank kept running back and forth getting things from the boot of the car. Then I saw the balloon in the sky and Daddy was shouting at everyone. I didn't know if this was another test or if we were really going to fly away. Mommy came and took me to the balloon and I stood in front of the big fire. I couldn't see anything but I could hear the fire. It sounded like a snake hissing. When I think about it, I can still hear the noise."

Frank and Peter used their sharp camping knives to cut the retaining cables, and the freedom balloon with its four passengers ascended at a speed of thirteen feet per second.

It was now one-thirty in the morning, Wednesday, July 4, 1979. The sky was overcast. A twenty-mile-an-hour wind blew from the north. The four fleeing refugees, two adults and two children, crouched together on the thin steel floor, over which they had spread a blanket so it wouldn't be so cold, as their balloon lifted them over the territory of East Germany. Later, they would find it hard to describe the sensation. "We had no sense of movement. Suspended in the air like that, we felt as if we were standing still, almost as if we were part of the wind itself."

After a few seconds, Frank looked down. "I was surprised that we were already as high up as we were. All I could make out were black woods outlined against the sky on the horizon."

Doris held Andreas close to her. "Now we were in the air I couldn't believe how quiet and smooth it was. I had imagined that it would be windy and jerky going up, and that I would get dizzy or nauseous. But we swung very slowly and very gently upward, as in a dream. I thought that it would be much more turbulent. I saw a few lights in the towns below. I guess they were street lights. Car headlights looked like glow-worms moving along the highway. I could tell that we were pretty high because the lights looked so small. Andreas trembled in my arms. It was very cold up there but I couldn't tell if he was shivering from fear or cold. I told him not to be afraid. I felt a wonderful sense of closeness to my family and had no doubt that we would make it."

Peter had to watch the flame the whole time to make sure that it didn't touch the cloth. He glanced at the altimeter once and remarked that they had already reached three thousand feet. Later he looked and saw that the indicator was stuck at 4,200 feet. "A spring must have snapped or something. Anyway, we no longer had an altimeter. . . ."

Shortly after takeoff, balloon captain Strelzyk had realized in horror that they had left two very important pieces of equipment on the ground below—the fire extinguisher and his heavy work gloves. "I had to hold the stovepipe exactly in the middle to prevent the cloth from catching fire. I couldn't relax for a second. The pipe wasn't quite long enough and if I hadn't held it upright, the outer edge of the fabric would have come in contact with the flame. That's why I had to concentrate so hard. The pipe was ice cold, less than twenty degrees Fahrenheit, because the gas that was released was cold until it caught fire at the end. I kept my hands on the metal for too long and they stuck to the pipe. When I tried to pull them away I left long strips of skin on the metal." At one point Doris held on to the pipe for support and later realized that she too had injured the palms of her hands. In the excitement at the time, neither of them noticed the pain.

Peter finally grabbed the pipe between his body and upper arm and continued to balance it exactly in the centre of the balloon opening. "I could still feel the cold pipe through my thick jacket and sweater though. Later it was terribly painful. But it would have been catastrophic if the fabric had caught fire. I knew enough about balloons to realize that fire was the worse thing that could happen. When a balloon catches fire, it catapults up in the air, sometimes to as high as 33,000 feet, and then when the cloth is completely burned up, the gondola carrying the passengers falls like a stone to the ground. . . ."

The family was in the air for ten minutes. Fifteen minutes. Twenty minutes. "I couldn't see anything on the ground any more," says Frank. "It was very dark and very scary."

Doris pressed her younger son to her body, hugged him, and stroked his hair. The child was quiet. Peter kept his eyes on the flame, making sure that it always remained exactly in the middle. And then it happened. . . .

About twenty-five minutes from takeoff, at an estimated altitude of 6,600 feet, disaster struck as the balloon hit the thick blanket of clouds. "Suddenly we were lost in fog and everything in the gondola was completely soaked," remembers Doris.

The town of Blankenstein in the German Democratic Republic. In the early morning hours of July 4, 1979, the Strelzyk family landed nearby, a few hundred yards from the mined "death strip".

For the first time the gondola started to jerk from side to side. A pocket of turbulence beneath the clouds grabbed the balloon and spun it around like a carousel. Then it was still again. Water from the atmosphere was quickly soaked up by the balloon, making the balloon several hundred pounds heavier. Peter regulated the gas flow to decrease the flame enough to bring the balloon below the clouds. Finally, they were out of the clouds and could see lights below them.

Relieved, the frightened passengers stared at the flame. They didn't notice that the balloon was still losing altitude.

Frank remembers what happened next. "I felt popping in my ears but I didn't remember it until much later. I just happened to look over the side and saw a few lights on the ground. They seemed much closer than they had been a few minutes before. I shouted at my father to look over the side."

Peter says, "I couldn't see a thing because I was completely blinded by the burner flame. I should have taken goggles with me."

Frank screamed, "Pop, I can see the trees!"

"We're sinking! Watch out!" yelled Doris.

But their warnings came too late. There was no time to reheat the air enough to raise the balloon. Frank says, "Suddenly the trees were at eye level. Then I heard the sound of the fabric ripping as the balloon caught on the trees."

Softly, unbelievably gently, the gondola pulled the balloon through the tall pine trees. The enormous shell caught in the tips of the trees, softening the impact as the gondola landed gently on the ground.

"It didn't seem real," says Doris today. "It was like a dream. No one panicked or screamed. Everything happened much too quickly. When we finally realized that we were on the ground again, it was too late to be afraid."

Peter told everyone to hold on and then ordered Frank to cut the guardrail so that they could get out of the gondola. One at a time—first Doris and Andreas, then Frank, and then Peter—they quickly jumped out of the gondola and ran about 150 feet through the woods to a safer spot.

"You don't stop to think in this kind of situation," explains Peter. "Instinct tells you what to do. Anything could have happened at that point. The propane bottles could have ex-

ploded or the balloon could have fallen on top of us, trap-
ping us in the gondola." But there was no explosion, no
noise. They stood in silence and waited.

The bewildered refugees found themselves in an unfa-
miliar forest and wondered if the surrounding trees belonged
to East or West Germany.

"The sixty-foot pine trees had slim, straight trunks and
thick crowns. As far as we could see in the dark, the
undergrowth seemed to have been cleared. The ground
under our feet was matted with a thick carpet of pine
needles. I could just make out what appeared to be two
hunter's blinds not too far away. But there was nothing to
tell me whether we were in East or West Germany. I still
didn't know if we had made it."

Peter turned to Frank and asked, "How long were we in
the air?"

"Exactly thirty-four minutes," answered Frank, looking at
the luminous dial of his watch.

"Then there's a good chance that we made it. Stay here
with your mother and Andreas while I try to find out where
we are."

Peter walked straight ahead for several hundred yards
under the covering of the thick roof of pine trees until he
reached the edge of the woods. In the dim twilight he was
able to discern some sort of fence about two hundred yards
ahead. He stepped back in alarm and stood straining his eyes
to make out the details. "Actually there were two fences,
each about fifteen feet high with a wide strip of land between them. I couldn't tell if this was just a harmless fence
or the border between East and West."

Still uncertain, Peter crept back to his family through the
dark woods. He tried to allay the fear that they all felt.
"We were in the air for thirty-four minutes so we must have
crossed the border long ago," he told his family. "The wind
velocity was at least twenty miles per hour and it was only
seven miles from our point of departure to the border. I
think we must be in West Germany." To himself he thought,
"But God help us if we're not. . . ."

They decided to move ahead all together and try to find
some clue which would tell them where they were. Slowly,

with Peter in the lead, they crept from tree to tree, eyes focused on the ground. They only used the flashlight when there was something in the way and then Peter held his hand over the light to dim the glare. They had been walking for several minutes when the beam fell on some strange spiral wires, winding along at waist height.

"Be careful! Wait!" whispered Peter. Carefully, he climbed over the high spiral only to discover a second one. Peter followed the second spiral slowly and then spotted a tree stump with a small box on it. The wire led to the box and on the other side of the stump there was another wire leading away from it. They had obviously stumbled across an alarm system—the type that triggered when a person or animal crossed the trip wire.

Peter says, "This discovery scared me but I tried to convince myself that maybe the West Germans did this as a safety measure so that no one would accidentally wander too close to the border. I had a feeling that I was wrong."

Even more cautious than before, he returned to his wife and children, who were waiting where he had left them, and informed them of his discovery. "We can't go any farther. We'll have to find some sort of clue first to tell us where we are."

Doris and Andreas stood still while Peter and Frank searched the ground with the flashlight. They found an empty beer bottle but the label was worn away and there was no brand name on it. Then Frank picked up the remains of a cellophane package. Quietly he called to his father. Frank stood in the small clearing, holding the transparent wrapper against the brightening sky. He could read the words "Toast Bread". His father came closer with the flashlight and, with difficulty, they deciphered the fine print word for word—"People's Owned Bakery, Wernigerode".

Peter quickly switched off the flashlight. "I thought my heart would stop. I knew we had failed. I couldn't believe that we were still in East Germany and that any moment border police with machine guns might appear and say, "Stop, or we'll shoot!"

10

The
Death
Strip

The fugitives had landed in the middle of the twilight zone that marked the border exactly two hundred yards from the mined death strip between East Germany and West Germany. Peter looked at his watch in the dawn light. It was shortly before four o'clock. "We'll have to hide somewhere until we can see a little better. Otherwise we run the risk of stumbling over a trip wire." He led the way again, stepping cautiously, never taking his eyes off the ground, like someone treading on thin ice. He was terrified that mines might be buried there.

About two hundred yards from where they had crashed, a short distance from where the balloon still hung in the trees like a beckoning flag, Peter—protecting his face with his hand—forced a path through the thick thorn bushes for himself and his family. They found a protective little hollow in the bushes and crouched down together to wait for daylight. "We all trembled from fear and the cold. I guess that's the way rabbits feel before the hunt begins."

Once more Peter embraced his wife and children, just as he had done before the takeoff. "Try not to be afraid," he said. "We'll get out of here. Somehow we'll make it. We have to get back to the car."

Today he admits, "What was I supposed to do? I knew, of course, that we didn't have a chance. But I couldn't let my family know that I was just as frightened as they were. I knew that there were watchtowers all over the place, that border police patrolled regularly. I also knew that the East German border stretched three miles inward, that trespassing here was strictly forbidden, and that anyone in the area was endangering his life. And I was aware of the fact that the sky was under radar surveillance. I was sure that our balloon must have been spotted on the radar screen as an unidentified object and that, when the object suddenly disappeared, it would have set off an alert. That's what was going through my head at the time anyway. I expected helicopters to begin a search as soon as it was light. On the other hand, we couldn't move until we could see where we were going."

Time passed slowly—fifteen minutes, thirty minutes, forty-five minutes. No one spoke. Andreas dozed in his mother's arms. Morning dewdrops dripped from the bushes and dampened their windcheaters. Birds started to chirp. The sky brightened in the east. No footsteps approached. They heard no voices or barking dogs in the distance, no helicopters in the sky above them.

Now that there was more light, Peter crept out of the bushes and studied his surroundings. He could see the wire spirals clearly now, weaving their way about a yard above the ground. He looked at the alarm boxes on the tree stumps which were clearly hooked up to the nearest watchtowers, where border police waited for an alarm to go off.

Hidden behind a bush at the edge of the woods, Peter stared at the western border of East Germany, at the high double fences separated by a minefield. He looked at the hilly countryside below, trying to get his bearings. They had landed on a sloping ridge which, as he later found out, was a foothill of the 2,390-foot Kulm mountain. From where he now stood he could see a little settlement on the East German side of the border, and on the horizon, on the other side of the border, he could see two West German villages. He later learned that the East German town was Blankenstein, and the West German towns were Langenbach and Lichtenberg.

The road leading from Lichtenberg in West Germany to Blankenstein in East Germany had been closed for more than thirty years. This area was particularly well guarded, as there was a watchtower every 550 to 1,000 yards. At night, spotlights illuminated a narrow path just wide enough for armoured cars to pass through. There were underground bunkers with observation slits. In several places there were mounds in front of unploughed control strips eleven yards wide. Behind these there were high grates or barbed-wire fences. Then came the mine belt and the second fence.

The automatic trip wires, funnel-shaped contraptions into which led cables and wires, were almost invisible to the unsuspecting. When someone tried to climb the fence, the contact wire triggered a fatal spray of lead bullets and splinters from the funnel. Many animals had been killed on the border by this apparatus.

Peter couldn't see everything in detail from where he stood, but he could see enough—the fences and the mine belt. "For a moment I considered attempting to climb the fence to the other side, but I knew it would be suicide. Alone, confused as I was, I might have tried it. But with my wife and children . . . I didn't want to endanger their lives any more than I already had. We had to try to get back to the car. It was our only chance."

Peter went back to his family and together they began their long retreat. Peter led the way, warning them repeatedly, "Careful! Wire! Don't step on it!" Frank followed his father, then came Andreas, and then Doris. They saw the last of the trip wires after they had walked about two hundred yards.

Relieved, the family stopped a moment to rest. The ground was slippery with morning dew and difficult to walk on. Roots stuck up out of the ground and there were small, deep ditches. Occasionally they heard the sound of a stream somewhere in the distance. They kept stepping in holes, tripping, and falling down. Andreas slipped and fell in a large puddle but he was concentrating so hard that he didn't even cry. "Daddy said that I shouldn't say a word and that I shouldn't cry because someone might hear me."

Peter used the compass, which he had put in his jacket pocket, to orientate himself. They marched directly north in the direction from which they had come. After a few hundred yards, directly in front of them, they spotted two small stone shelters surrounded by barbed wire—watch huts for the border troops. They stopped dead in their tracks and waited. But there was no one around. "Our comrades must have been sleeping on the job that morning," says Peter today, grinning.

They detoured cautiously as they had already done many times. "It was a nerve-wracking, extremely tiring obstacle course—three steps forward, two back, three sideways, look for cover under bushes and trees, go around another obstacle, and again a few yards forward. It took us almost an hour for the first six hundred yards. We had to be extremely careful because guards might appear at any moment."

And so they continued until they reached an unploughed potato field. "We were pretty exhausted by that time and this completely open, unprotected field presented a new danger. Again we waited awhile, observing the area carefully."

While they were resting, the sun rose above the treetops in the Thuringian Forest. For the fugitives it was much too soon. It was already so light that they could see minute details five hundred yards away.

Peter told his family, "We have no choice. We have to get across the potato field as quickly as possible. But don't run. We don't want to draw attention to ourselves." In single file they marched, cutting diagonally across the field in a furrow. Andreas fell down several times and his mother helped him back to his feet.

From the middle of the field they could see a narrow asphalt road ahead and heard the sound of an engine in the distance. Peter gave a signal and they threw themselves face down in the furrow. The green leaves of the potato plants hid them from view.

Frank risked a look up and saw a truck on the road ahead.

It was too far away to tell if it was a military or civilian vehicle. But as the car came closer, Peter recognized it as a W-50, an agricultural vehicle manufactured in Ludwigs-felde, East Germany.

The truck drove by without seeing them. The family bent over to avoid detection and hurried to the nearby woods. They paused here to catch their breath and then continued farther north along the edge of the woods. At 6 A.M. they approached a sign on a red-and-yellow post which read: "*Border!* Trespassing and entering strictly forbidden!"

Finally! They had left the three-mile death strip behind them. About a half mile farther down the road, just as they reached Neuendorfer, several National People's Army jeeps came into view ahead of them. The Strelzyks threw themselves in the nearest bushes and watched as the jeeps passed them a few yards away.

They hurried on, walking east on a main road. The sun warmed their faces and dried their damp clothes. About a mile farther down the road, houses came into view and they passed a sign indicating that they had reached Loben-stein.

Lobenstein is a tiny town on the border with a population of about five thousand, most of whom work in the tobacco and leather factories in the town's immediate vicinity. Trav-ellers pass through Lobenstein on their way to the Hirsch-berg checkpoint, arriving from the Berlin Hof Autobahn. It was here, two years before, that an Italian truck driver, a member of the Italian Communist Party, was mistakenly shot down by German border police when he climbed down from his truck to take a walk near the border.

It was already 7 A.M. and the streets of Lobenstein were bustling. The Strelzyks brushed the dirt from their clothes and tried to look as though they were tourists out for an early morning walk. (This was not an uncommon sight, as many tourists camp in the Bleiloch valley and hike in the morning.)

Peter noticed several official-looking vehicles, Wolgas with aerials on the roofs. He also saw an unusual number of pedestrians with the Party emblem on their jackets. He remembered hearing once that people living right on the border had to be Party members in good standing, because officials assumed that they would be less likely to try to escape.

The Strelzyks felt more secure now that they were in the crowded town. They walked along Highway 90 going north again and saw nothing but a few tractors and hay wagons. Peter was beginning to think that they might make it back to the car after all.

They continued on for another three miles and turned onto a path in the woods shortly before Heinersdorf. Now they were less than nine hundred yards from their point of departure, from the hidden clearing in the woods. Just as Peter was sure that they had overcome every obstacle, a tow truck with "Auto Repair Lobenstein" painted on the side passed them and turned into the very path they wanted to take. "Damn," thought Peter. "Now they're going to take our car away from us."

Assuming that the police would already be in the clearing, Peter considered turning back. "I was sure that they had the area surrounded though, and decided to take a chance. We moved very slowly from one tree to the next. When we finally reached the clearing, there was no one else around and the tow truck was nowhere to be seen. All we could hear were the birds chirping in the trees."

It was now 8:30 A.M.—eight hours since they had left from this exact spot in their balloon headed for the West. The scene had not changed. The only difference was that now everything was bathed in bright sunlight. The Moskwitsch stood in the field facing the same southerly direction. The bonnet was still open and the cables still led from the battery to the cold air blower with which they had filled the balloon. The blowtorch was on the ground, still connected to the two propane bottles. The right back door of the car was still open—as if Doris had just now lifted her son Andreas from the back seat. The trailer that had carried the balloon was still attached to the car.

"Hurry," called Peter. "Just throw everything in the trailer. We have to get out of here right away." Within five minutes all traces of the attempted escape had disappeared from the clearing. Blowtorch, blower, and propane bottles were thrown in the trailer. The tarpaulin was pulled across and snapped. The four Strelzyks got in the car, slammed the doors, and drove away.

Peter took the path back to the main road leading to Pössneck. A vehicle with a blue light on the roof approached them from the opposite direction. Doris was on the verge of panic until she saw that it was an ambulance on its way from an accident.

Peter did not take the direct route back to Pössneck. He made a detour shortly before Gosswitz, high above the Hohenwarte valley, and turned into a side street where he stopped the car in front of a concealed garbage dump. He and Frank unloaded the blowtorch, cold air blower, motorcycle engine, iron poles, and butane burner from the trailer, and threw them on the heap of refuse.

They reached Pössneck at nine-thirty. Peter remembers thinking, "Everything has gone well up to now but when we get home, the police or State Security will be waiting there for us. Someone must have seen the car in the clearing and reported the number."

But no one was waiting for them—no one but the grey, white, and brown house cat, Purzel, who wandered from the backyard to greet them. Purring happily, she rubbed up against the dirty trouser legs of the returning balloonists.

Another view of the wooded area where the Strelzyk family landed on July 4, 1979. The family did not know if it had landed in the East or the West until the elder boy discovered an empty package with an East German brand name on it.

11

The Cover-up

The Strelzyks returned to their house exhausted and disappointed. "It was strange, as if we were just visiting," says Doris. "Everything was as clean and neat as I had left it. But somehow I felt as if I were seeing it for the first time." She undressed Andreas, who was in a daze, and patted his face with a wet face cloth before putting him to bed. She closed the curtain and he fell asleep immediately. Frank was exhausted too and went to bed without being told. He quickly fell into a deep, dreamless sleep.

Peter wanted to be alone. He closed the bedroom door, sat down on the edge of the bed, and buried his face in both hands. "I sobbed. I was completely out of control. I don't think I had ever been so shaken. I realized then that my nerves were shot. Over and over, I kept thinking, 'Only two hundred yards . . . a few more seconds in the air and we would have been in the West—not here in Pössneck where, any moment now, there would be a knock at the door and the Stasi or Vopos would be standing there.' That it was only two hundred yards, that's what got to me. Two miles would have been easier to accept. But we had been so close to freedom. . . ."

It took Peter thirty minutes to get himself under control so that he could think clearly again. Then it occurred to him that his wife and children needed alibis. Doris hadn't shown up at the bank and the children were absent from school. (No one was expecting Peter anywhere because he had told all his customers that he was taking a holiday.)

Doris, who was initially better able to cope with the shock and disappointment of the experience, was calmer than Peter. Peter says, "My hands shook all day. I drank gallons of coffee and smoked constantly." But Doris was contained enough to write—in clear, even handwriting—an excuse for Frank to his class teacher:

> Dear Mrs. Drechsler,
>   My son Frank has the flu and I have kept him home from school today. He'll be back as soon as he's better.
>   Thank you very much.
>   Sincerely,
>   Doris Strelzyk

Doris delivered the note personally later that morning to the school. The teacher was understanding and wished Frank a speedy recovery.

Later Peter drove Andreas and Doris to the pediatrician, Dr. Mohorn. "We thought that this would double as an excuse for Doris not to go to the bank. She could say that she had to stay home to take care of her sick child. And, to tell the truth, he really didn't look well that day. He had caught cold during the night, and was pale and coughing."

They waited nearly an hour before the doctor had time to examine the child. He diagnosed a slight case of flu, prescribing some medicine and a few days of rest in bed.

Peter dropped Andreas and Doris off at home and drove into town alone. He went to the Pössneck Savings Bank on Breiten Street and excused his wife's absence: "Our little boy, Andreas, is sick and was up all night coughing. My wife would have called this morning but she had to take him to the doctor. She won't be in today." They said that they hoped to see Doris back on the job the next day.

It was already noon. Doris prepared chicken for lunch but

no one could eat. The two children pushed the food around on their plates and Peter didn't touch his. Exhausted, the four of them finally went to bed. The children slept right away. Doris tossed and turned in bed. "I was so upset that I woke up every few minutes in a cold sweat. I dreamt that we landed somewhere with the balloon and climbed out. A car drove up to us and men in uniforms jumped out—National People's Army uniforms. They pointed guns at us. . . ."

Peter, too, had a hard time finding peace that afternoon. He bathed, put on pyjamas, and went to bed. But sleep evaded him. He got up and paced back and forth in the living room—the room he had wallpapered himself and had been so proud of, the room that now seemed to him like a prison cell. He paced up and down, eight steps in one direction and eight back. Then he sat in the easy chair and chain-smoked. "I cried more that day than the rest of my life put together. The physical exhaustion was only part of it. I could take that. But what got to me was the depression. I felt like a man lost at sea in a small boat, who at last sees land ahead. Then suddenly the wind changes and pushes the boat back out to sea. . . ."

Peter had always been a self-confident man, used to solving problems at work and in his personal life. He had never tasted failure. "I was proud of the relatively high standard of living which I had provided for my family. But I knew that I had gone as far as possible in East Germany. Now my only wish, the only challenge for me, was freedom. All I wanted was to be a free man in the West. And I had failed. Why had I picked this time to fail, when so much depended on it? Just a few seconds more, and we would have made it. If I'd been more careful, we wouldn't have hit the clouds. It was my fault. I had failed."

For the first time in his life, Peter knew how it felt to be a loser. His body shook in silent sobs. "It was the hopelessness of the situation that was so shattering. As long as we had a balloon in the basement, ready to go, it gave me hope. It symbolized my being able to get my family out of East Germany. Now my hopes were in shreds. Everything seemed senseless and hollow, even life itself. I knew that I was on the verge of a breakdown."

All afternoon Peter remained alone in his bedroom with his thoughts. Outside his room, life in Socialist Germany went on as usual. The regional Branch of the Party was organizing a propaganda meeting for the upcoming anniversary celebration. This week's theme was "Strong ties to the Communist Party of the Soviet Union: the foundation of our present and future success as a Socialist society." Attendance at the meeting was mandatory for all factory propagandists, agitators, and lecturers. The Progress Soccer Team was playing a pre-season practice game against the neighbouring town's team, Motor Zeulenroda. That evening the local Free German Youth organization was sponsoring another festive dance with a disco at Sound 2000.

The Strelzyks, with the exception of Andreas who was still sound asleep, sat down at the dinner table early that evening. Suddenly Frank said loudly, "Hey, Pop, did you bring the IDs and photos back or are they still in the gondola?" Peter was horrified. He hadn't even thought about them. But Doris calmed him down. "Don't get excited. I brought everything back."

They tried to remember if they might have left anything else in the gondola which would lead to them. "We left the first-aid kit," said Frank. "And the butane lamp. But no one could trace them back to us. They wouldn't have a clue as to where they came from." Peter agreed and tried not to worry.

After dinner they sat in the living room in front of the television set. Peter switched nervously from East to West channels trying to find something entertaining enough to distract him.

He found nothing but news on TV: the so-called Innovator Collectives reported a 29 billion mark profit through creative performance in factories for the period from 1971 to 1978. In Berlin, the secretaries responsible for international and ideological questions concerning various Socialist and Worker parties were meeting for the first time. Erich Honecker, East Germany's president, congratulated James Earl Carter, president of the U.S.A., on his country's national holiday.

The main theme in West Germany was the decision to

nominate Franz Josef Strauss as Christian Democratic candidate for chancellor. The president of the Federal Employment Agency, Josef Stingl, said that recent figures showed a further reduction in unemployment. The Frankfurt Stock Exchange announced that the stock market indicated a stable trend toward recovery.

The weather, which had been unusually bad that summer, was taking a turn for the better. Sunshine and temperatures higher than seventy-five degrees Fahrenheit were predicted for both parts of Germany.

And in the little town of Pössneck, another lovely summer day was drawing to an end. It was slightly cloudy but warm and pleasant. The mercury had risen to seventy-three degrees that day. The clouds were gone by the time the sun disappeared behind the Thuringian mountains and the red glow of the sunset was reflected in the windows of the old houses in the marketplace.

All this was lost on the Strelzyks, however, as they sat in the living room and discussed their abortive escape. "Actually, we were damned lucky. It could have been much worse. At least we had all made it back safe and sound. Imagine if we had landed in the middle of the mine belt," said Doris.

Frank agreed with his mother. "The flight wasn't all that bad. Considering that it was our first try, we did pretty well. If we had noticed sooner that we were sinking, then we could have raised the flame and we would have made it. We had enough propane to make it."

After a pause in the conversation, fifteen-year-old Frank said quietly, "Pop, do you think the Stasi are looking for us now?"

"Probably. They must have found the balloon by now. And if so, then they'll be out looking for the people who tried to escape in it."

Doris added, "They'll act as if we committed murder or something. They'll follow every possible clue. Once they've found the giant balloon, they'll try to find out where all that fabric was bought. I'm worried that they'll eventually find something that leads them to us. Sooner or later they're bound to find us. . . ."

The three stared at each other for several minutes in silence.

Then Frank said, "I think there's only one thing to do. We'll just have to build another balloon. . . ."

12

Fugitives in Berlin

Frank was the first to put into words what Peter had been thinking about since early that evening. "Try again with a new balloon—that was really our last and only chance. We knew now that, in principle, the balloon functioned. We had had a smooth takeoff, an easy flight, and even landed safely. Technically everything was as it should have been. We had just been victims of bad luck."

That very evening Peter told Doris and Frank, "The next time we'll just be luckier. That's all there is to it." His depression lifted as they started to work on new plans that night, trying to come up with the best and easiest way to get new material for a balloon.

Peter knew that it would cost close to 20,000 marks for fabric and other material. Like most hardworking East German citizens, the Strelzyks had a fairly large amount of money in their savings account. "It was easy to save money because many of us were earning high wages and we had little to spend it on. The supply shortage was such that we couldn't buy what we wanted even when we had the money. So everything went into our savings accounts."

But Peter still worked twenty-hour days during the next

few weeks to earn additional money. He resumed his business as if nothing had happened, laying new home wiring and repairing cable systems in old buildings. "Conditions in the older Pössneck homes were gruesome. I often found raw, uninsulated wiring in the apartments." Peter moonlighted or, more accurately, worked "after hours" (illegal work is nonexistent in East Germany) at various other odd jobs.

Several days after the unsuccessful flight, Peter decided to get rid of his old orange Moskwitsch. "I still felt uneasy when I was driving the car. I couldn't stop thinking that someone might have seen it parked at our launching site and written down the number. I sold it as quickly as I could to the State Supply Exchange for 2,800 marks. It was such an ancient model that no one wondered why I was selling it."

A few days later he bought an old Wartburg 311 from his brother-in-law, Horst Städter, a driving instructor in Pössneck. "It was still in pretty good condition and not bad looking, blue with a white roof. The engine was in tiptop shape and I repaired a few minor things myself."

Doris, who at first had been relatively calm and unshaken by their attempted escape, grew more and more apprehensive about their present situation as time passed. "I was afraid to walk past policemen on the street. I was even afraid to answer the doorbell. I tried to stay calm but I was jumpy and nervous all the time. I guess I was just paranoid."

When the children weren't around, Doris and Peter discussed what the authorities must be doing since they had discovered the balloon. Peter knew. "With the possible exception of murder, there's no worse crime in East Germany than fleeing the Republic. I knew that the Vopos and Stasi would organize a major search for anyone who was daring enough to try to escape in a balloon."

Official reaction to the balloon caper can only be reconstructed in fragments today. Surprisingly enough, the torn balloon hanging in the trees was not discovered by a patrol until twenty-four hours after the crash. Police immediately searched the area and found nothing. They alerted the nearest Border Police Headquarters located near Lobenstein, as well as the National People's Army in Wurzbach. Hundreds of soldiers using trained dogs combed the area between

Hirschberg in the east and Sonnenberg in the west. Low-flying helicopters scanned the treetops searching for clues. Radar stations in the border area were queried but they reported nothing unusual on the screens. Even the agricultural pilots were questioned.

The State Security Service in Gera, in the centre of the city on Tordurchgang Street, was informed. The "firm" (as East Germans sometimes call the State Security Service) was located in an old house that had formerly belonged to a wealthy Gera citizen. The official sign next to the entrance said "State Security Ministry". Net curtains barely succeeded in hiding the bars on the windows from passersby on the street.

The Gera State Security Service passed on the information they had collected to the Central State Security Service in Berlin by radio. Specialists from the capital arrived the same day at the scene of the "crime". They carefully freed the balloon and the gondola from the trees and carried it away from the border in an army jeep. Local inhabitants were asked vague questions but no mention was made to them of the balloon. Even later, when the People's Police asked the public's help in solving a "serious crime", the fact that the crime involved an attempted escape in a hot-air balloon was kept secret.

Peter says, "We heard some gossip about a search but never any details. Suspense hung over our heads like the sword of Damocles."

School holidays began on July 14 and the Strelzyks decided to drive to East Berlin. "We were mainly interested in getting away from Pössneck, but we also planned to buy material for the new balloon in the capital. We figured that the stores there would have more in stock than elsewhere. We had friends there and thought that visiting them might take our minds off our problems."

Peter telephoned ahead to reserve a room in the renowned Stadt Berlin Hotel on Alexanderplatz. "We didn't want to stay with friends or relatives because we were afraid that they might be implicated in our escape if we were caught later."

Early in the morning on Saturday, July 14, the whole family set out for Berlin in the newly acquired Wartburg. The two boys seemed to have survived the attempted escape with no ill effects. "Andreas hardly mentioned it any more and we were careful to make sure he understood that he was never to say a word about it outside the family."

The new car didn't take them very far. On the main road leading out of Pössneck, Neustadter Street, the engine broke down. They stopped at a filling station but there was no mechanic on duty and Peter couldn't fix it himself. "I knew that the one person who could help me right away was Günter Wetzel, but we had agreed not to see each other. I didn't want to have to tell him about our failure because I knew how disappointed he would be."

But realizing that Günter was probably the only one who could save his Berlin holiday, Peter drove the car to Tuchmacher Street. Günter greeted the surprise visitors heartily and asked no unnecessary questions. He started to work on the engine immediately and within thirty minutes he had fixed it. The problem had been a cylinder head. Then he wished them a pleasant trip and they left.

Peter drove through the scenic Orla valley, via Neustadt to the Triptis Autobahn entrance. They crossed over the Leipzig Autobahn and took the Dessau-Wittenburg exit to the sign pointing to Magdeburg in the west and Frankfurt an der Oder in the east (to be distinguished from the major city of Frankfurt am Main in West Germany). They reached the Berlin beltway at noon and took it straight into the centre of the city to Alexanderplatz, where they saw the sun mirrored on the giant globe on the East Berlin television tower.

They parked the car at the hotel and looked up at the nearly forty storey skyscraper, Interhotel Stadt Berlin, where they were to spend their holiday.

"It was so elegant," remembers Frank, "that I felt sort of self-conscious going in." The guests from the province were taken to a room on the thirty-fifth floor with television, wall-to-wall carpeting, and a luxury bathroom. The room cost 120 marks a night.

The Strelzyks spent the next day sleeping late, relaxing,

and strolling through the streets of the capital of East Germany. They promenaded along Unter den Linden in the sunshine and saw the famous Brandenburg Gate in the distance. They walked across the windy avenues, some of which are so wide that pedestrians look tiny and lost on them. They visited stores on Alexanderplatz and gazed at the world clock that symbolized the international relations developed by East Germany.

The city was plastered with posters for the forthcoming anniversary celebration. The number 30 was displayed in department stores, on walls of buildings, and on banners everywhere:

30 years GDR: our Republic is the true home of the people.

Excellent performance in Socialist Emulation in honour of the 30th anniversary of the GDR.

We are proud in honour of the 30th anniversary: eternal friendship with the Soviet Union, the life force of the GDR.

On Unter den Linden, banners reminiscent of a West German election campaign waved in the wind proclaiming "Security, Solidarity, Protection!" Only the emblem of East Germany with its wreath of wheat and its hammer and sickle made it clear that this was the advertising of the East German nation.

Berliners, known for their sharp, biting humour in both West and East Berlin, responded to the slogans with subtle jokes. The main topic of conversation was the supply shortage which, for some unknown reason, seemed even worse in this celebration year than in normal times. One East German joke, said to have originated in East Berlin, described the conditions in this way: a man comes into the underwear department of the Central Department Store on Alexanderplatz, sees nothing but empty shelves, and asks the salesperson, "Are you sold out of underpants here?" The salesperson answers, "No, I'm afraid you're in the wrong aisle. They're sold out of underpants over there in the next aisle. Here we're sold out of under*shirts*."

The Strelzyks were faced with their own supply shortage
in Berlin. There was no airtight material in the department
stores. Nowhere could they find the lightweight, inexpensive
tafetta they needed for their new balloon. One day after
visiting friends in Pankow they went to the House of Fabric,
which was surrounded by a construction fence. A sign on the
fence assured "Business as usual during renovation." But
again the Strelzyks were disappointed. They went to several
other shops and department stores but always in vain. It
seemed that the supply shortage was no joke.

After a few days, discouragement set in. "It was obvious
that we would never be able to get all the material from one
store this time. We had to assume that the Stasi had alerted
all the "speciality" shops in East Germany and that anyone,
anywhere, wanting to buy an unusually large amount of
taffeta at one time would be reported. Then, when we found
that we couldn't even find what we wanted in small quantities in Berlin, we started to lose hope. . . ."

Arriving back at the hotel garage one evening after a drive
through the city, Peter suddenly had a new idea. He had
noticed a conspicuous number of automobiles with diplomatic licence plates on the streets of the city and they
brought to mind a film he had seen on West German television. "The movie came back to me in detail. It was all about
East German citizens who were being smuggled to West
Berlin in diplomatic cars. I was desperate enough to try anything and began to work out a plan in my head. An escape in
a balloon would have been spectacular, but I really didn't
care about being a hero. I just wanted to get out of the
country as quickly and with as little risk as possible. Maybe
I could find help in diplomatic circles."

The view from the Strelzyks' room on the thirty-fifth floor
was especially impressive at night. Below them lay Alexanderplatz, the centre of the East German capital into which
wide, impersonal boulevards (typical of East Bloc cities)
converge. Beyond this, it was dark, with only a few street
lamps intermittently lighting the ruins near the wall.

When darkness fell, powerful spotlights drenched the
Wall that "protected the GDR from imperialism" in glaring
light. From the windows of the Interhotel Stadt Berlin, this

ugly, angular structure looked like a snake winding its way through the divided city, with the bright neon lights of West Berlin flickering beyond it. It was while looking out the window at this view that Peter made up his mind to contact the representative in East Berlin of the United States of America.

What happened in the following few days could have come straight out of a cheap spy movie. Early in the evening of July 17, Peter left his room, took the lift to the lobby, and left the hotel. He meandered over to the East Berlin television tower across the street, trying to look like a tourist out for a stroll but furtively glancing over his shoulder several times to make sure that he wasn't being followed. He entered a public telephone booth, took a scrap of paper out of his pocket, and dialled the number 222-27-41. It was several minutes before a man's voice on the other end of the line said, "Embassy of the United States of America."

Peter spoke softly and clearly, stressing the sentences which he had carefully prepared in advance. "We're being hunted! Please help us!" Then he gave his hotel and room number. He thought that the line might be tapped, but that was a risk he had to take.

After a short pause the man's voice answered in German with an American accent. "The Embassy is closed. Please call again tomorrow."

Peter hung the telephone back on the hook and quickly left the booth. He was disappointed by the cold, unconcerned response to his plea but told himself that they had no choice. They would have to react that way. He was sure that they would find a way to contact him.

Peter spent the rest of the evening in his room waiting for a call or some sort of signal. Nervously, he smoked one cigarette after the other. He waited that night, the following day, and the night after that. But nothing happened.

When he went down to the lobby Thursday evening, he instructed Doris to stay by the phone in the room. He stood in the lobby and watched the East German and foreign guests hurrying back and forth. He bought a *Neues Deutschland* newspaper and sat down in an easychair with a glass-top table in front of it.

He skimmed the paper: "Increased Productivity Through Science and Technology" announced the headline. The article elaborated on successful harvests, reconstruction efforts, and the military power and combat readiness of GDR troops. The television guide listed part one of a nine-part series entitled *The Decisive Front*, about the war in the Caucasus. *The Battle of the Panzers* would also be on television that week.

Peter had just dropped the newspaper in his lap when a man walked straight across the lobby toward him and asked in German, with an American accent, "Is anyone sitting next to you?" Peter answered by shaking his head. He camouflaged himself behind his newspaper and watched the stranger from the corner of his eyes. "He looked American. He was dressed like an American."

The man, about forty-five years old, was wearing an expensive black leather jacket with light-coloured trousers and an open sports shirt. Peter was sure that this was his contact. "He watched me from the corner of his eye just as I watched him but he seemed hesitant to speak. I was afraid to make the first move because, as everyone knows, the lobby of the Interhotel Stadt Berlin is overrun with secret police."

Peter acted like one who had seen too many late night spy movies. He fiddled with his hotel key and, pretending to be casual, placed it on the table so that the man seated next to him could clearly read the number 3507.

"He looked at the key. Then he looked me straight in the eye and I returned the look."

Demonstratively, or so it seemed to Peter, the man lit an American Marlboro. It smelled very much to Peter like the "air of freedom and adventure" in the German advertisements for this cigarette brand. After five or ten minutes had gone by, the stranger stood up, walking slowly to the bank of lifts on the other side of the lobby, and got in the one which only went to those floors above the twentieth. Certain that the man was on his way to room 3507, Peter took the next lift to his floor, rushed into the room, and asked Doris, "Where is he? Was there a man here? Did anyone knock?" Confused, Doris answered, "No. Why do you ask? No one's been here."

Disappointed, Peter ran across the carpeted hallway back to the lift, and rode back down to the lobby where he again saw the American. The man saw him too, stood for a moment looking at Peter, and then slowly walked to the hotel entrance. Peter followed, staying several steps behind him.

"I felt as if everyone in the lobby were staring at me. But it was probably my imagination." Peter stood behind the glass door of the hotel and watched from a distance as the man in the leather jacket got into a green Lada limousine parked in the adjacent lot. Instead of going directly to the main street, the Lada slowly approached the hotel driveway. Peter waited tensely at the door. "I could hardly contain myself when I saw the diplomatic number on the car."

Uncertain what was expected of him, Peter waited. The car came closer to the entrance and drove slowly past him without stopping, continuing on to the main road where it disappeared in the Berlin traffic. Peter walked toward the road and stood cursing to himself. Had he bungled? Should he have spoken to the American, or perhaps followed him to the car?

Once again he called the embassy. This time the party on the other end hung up on him. Peter went back to his room to wait for a call from the American. But the phone never rang—not that night, nor the following morning or afternoon. All things considered, Peter felt that the Americans had let him down.

And so Peter made yet another attempt to recruit aid from diplomatic circles. This time he went to another political adversary of East Germany—the People's Republic of China.

"Maybe the Red Chinese will help me if I offer them something in return," thought Peter. "And I'm going to put it in writing to make sure that they understand my position."

He borrowed a portable Erika typewriter from the hotel reception desk, took it to his room, and using one finger, he typed his plea to the Embassy of the People's Republic of China: "We're being hunted! Please help us! On the night of July 3 we attempted to escape East Germany in a hot-air balloon but landed 200 yards on this side of the border. We are enemies of the State. We beg you to help us: husband, thirty-seven years old, electrician; wife, thirty-one years old, clerk; son, fifteen years old, student; son, eleven years old, student. In payment for your help we are willing to live and work in your country for three years without wages. Please help us! Interhotel Stadt Berlin, room 3507."

Peter folded the letter as small as possible and put it in a cigarette pack with only one cigarette in it. He carefully closed the pack and put it in the side pocket of his jacket.

The next day, July 20, he and his family walked to Pankow where they had been invited by friends for coffee. On their way, they passed the Pankow Public Swimming Pool situated between Schloss Park and Wolfshagener Street. In nice weather some 20,000 visitors come here to relax and enjoy the scenery in the park. It was a sunny day and Andreas asked if he and his brother could come back after coffee and go for a swim. Peter answered that they had better things to do that day.

After visiting their friends, Peter used a map of Berlin he had bought earlier to guide them to the "anti-imperialist Wall". They wandered along the edge of the Wall for about an hour until they reached Heinrich Mann Street, a dead-end leading directly to the Wall and the Embassy of the People's Republic of China.

The street was desolate and the three-storey embassy building was surrounded by ruins. The embassy was painted a nondescript yellow and topped with a tile roof. A fence, slightly higher than a grown man, surrounded the neglected garden which extended about 3,500 square yards. There was a wide staircase leading to the entrance with a small showcase next to it. Peter pretended to be interested in the pictures of MIG fighter planes and Soviet-type panzers with Chinese characters painted on them. "Army of the People's Republic of China" was written in German underneath the pictures.

Peter looked around carefully. In the light of the low-lying evening sun, he saw a greyish-green watchtower directly in front of the Wall about 160 yards away. An East German border soldier with a shoulder rifle was posted there. Peter walked a few yards along the embassy fence, turned his back to the soldier, reached into his pocket, and took out the cigarette pack. He removed the one cigarette, lit it, closed the pack with the note still in it, and threw it with a quick twist of his wrist through the iron bars into the embassy yard.

The pack with the hidden message fell about two yards behind the fence in the high weeds. Peter turned toward his wife and children, standing a few feet behind him, and saw that the East German soldier had apparently been facing his direction when he had thrown the cigarette pack. "I could feel the adrenalin pulsing through my veins. I had to control myself not to run."

Briskly, but not too quickly, Peter started to walk away, arm in arm with Doris, followed by Frank and Andreas. "I expected to feel a hand on my shoulder any minute. I was petrified that the guard had seen me and the message in the cigarette pack would give everything away."

They arrived at a bus stop but Peter was too impatient to wait, so they walked on. The more distance they put between themselves and the embassy, the calmer Peter felt. They finally reached the hotel without being stopped.

Peter threw himself on his bed in the hotel room. "We were so afraid that the message would land in the wrong hands. It was practically a signed confession."

He finally calmed down enough to dial the number of the Red Chinese embassy—480-0161. A woman's voice answered in Chinese.

Peter asked if she spoke German.

"Yes, a little."

Slowly, emphasizing each word, he said, "Please look outside in your yard. There's a cigarette pack just inside the fence with an important message for you. . . ." Then he hung up.

In the meantime, Andreas had switched on the television. The sound of combat fire came from the speaker, and panzers rolled across the screen. The war serial, *The Decisive Front*, was being shown on the East German channel.

Doris called room service and had a snack sent up to the

room. Shortly after ten o'clock the telephone rang. Peter tore the receiver from the phone.

"Yes, this is room 3705."

Silence on the other end. Nothing but silence for several minutes. "Then," says Peter, "I clearly heard breathing and soft music in the background. I kept saying hello—until a couple of minutes later the receiver was hung up on the other end. It was very strange. I was sure that I had heard Chinese music in the background."

Frank said, "They're probably afraid that it's a hoax. They wanted to find out if there was an answer at the number you gave them. They'll probably call back."

And in fact the mysterious caller did call back. The telephone rang three separate times that night. Each time it was the same. Peter would answer the phone and hear nothing but breathing and soft Chinese music in the background. Then the caller would hang up. Peter was so nervous that he couldn't stop shaking. Instead of trying to sleep, he sat up until late that night drinking coffee and chain-smoking, ready to jump for the telephone. Finally, impatience overcame him and he dialled the embassy for the second time.

"This is 3507. Please answer me. Say something!"

But although the phone at the other end was picked up, there was complete silence. Peter interpreted the silence as confirmation that it was indeed the embassy that had made the previous calls. Red China didn't talk.

They got up at six o'clock the next morning. Only the children had slept. Doris and Peter had been awake all night looking out the window at the dark city below them.

The telephone rang. Chinese music. No one spoke.

"We couldn't figure out what was going on, whether they were really trying to reach us, or if someone was playing a trick on us, or trying to frighten us."

Peter and Doris were disconcerted. They hastily packed their things, checked out of the luxury hotel, and left Berlin heading south on the Autobahn.

"I felt like someone who had stumbled into quicksand. I was fighting to get out, but just kept getting deeper and deeper. . . ."

They left the Autobahn at Triptis and took the highway back through the Orla valley to Pössneck, passing long fields of wheat where combine harvesters were already at work. The harvest had begun in the fields of the Agricultural Co-operatives of Thuringia. The local paper was able to report: "Combine captains are doing a superb job. To date, corn losses have been kept to under one percent."

13

The
Evidence
Mounts

They arrived back home on the day of the annual town fair. Carousels and booths were already set up on the town periphery, and Frank asked if they could get out of the car and go to the fair. Peter agreed but reminded both children once again not to say a word to anyone about what had happened in East Berlin.

Peter said later that he felt like a stranger in his hometown when he arrived back from the capital. "I suddenly noticed things that I had never consciously seen before. For instance, a sign on a furniture factory: 'Production goal: 1,012 living room sets and 16,640 tables.'" He continued on through the cobblestone streets as fast as he could.

They drove by the marketplace and saw a couple of Young Pioneers standing near the fountain carrying rolled-up red flags under their arms. They were probably on their way from a routine weekend rally.

They arrived at the house on Altenburg Circle and unloaded the luggage from the car. "I felt as if everyone in the neighbourhood were watching us, and imagined how the neighbours would react if they had known that we were trying to escape to the West."

They were, after their experience in Berlin, now fully convinced that there was only one escape route open. "We knew
that we would have to build a third balloon, but I also knew
that I couldn't handle it alone. I would have to ask Günter to
help us."

From August 1978, when he backed out of the balloon
project, until May 1979, Günter Wetzel had worked for the
Pössneck Polyclinic as a driver. "Actually I was sort of a man
Friday for anything having to do with motors and cars,"
Günter recalled. He chauffeured the doctors in a Wolga limousine, drove the ambulance occasionally, and at one time or
another, worked on every vehicle in the car park. "I can
never say no when people ask me to do favours for them. So I
guess they took advantage of my good nature when I worked
there. Sometimes I found myself working seventy or eighty
hours a week."

He quit that job in May for a better-paying job as a driver
at People's Owned Trucking and Transport, delivering furniture in a Czech Skoda truck from the factory to shops
throughout East Germany. His job had taken him all the
way to Rostock, Schwerin, Güstrow, and sometimes as far as
Frankfurt an der Oder and East Berlin, and had taught him
the network of East German highways. "To tell the truth, I
enjoyed the travelling, but it was depressing to see how many
trucks lay around unused because there were no spare parts."

Working by himself in his spare time, he had completely
finished repairs on the outside of his house on Tuchmacher
Street, and had most recently installed a new front door.
Once a week he went to the gym and lifted weights for the
Pössneck Progress Team. "I wasn't very ambitious about
sports, but it was fun, and it gave me a chance to socialize
with a few friends and co-workers."

Andreas, the Wetzels' younger son, was now two years old
and attended a day-care centre in Pössneck. Petra picked
him up in the afternoons and he usually spent the rest of the
day playing with neighbourhood children in the backyard.

With Günter on the road much of the time and Andreas
becoming less dependent on her, Petra was left with more
time for herself. She often pondered on their decision to

drop out of the balloon project, and was no longer convinced that they had done the right thing. "Several incidents had occurred which made me decide that I really didn't want to spend the rest of my life in East Germany."

On Monday, July 23, Günter was surprised to see his old friend Peter standing at the new front door. Günter had heard rumours about the discovery of a balloon near Lobenstein, and had hoped that Peter would contact him so that he could find out if it had been their balloon and, if so, what had gone wrong. He was pleased and excited to see Peter at the door, but before they had a chance to say anything, something happened to postpone their discussion.

They heard the heart-rending screams of a child from a corner of the yard and ran out to see what was wrong. Andreas, blood streaming down his face, was writhing on the ground sobbing. He and his five-year-old brother had fallen from their scooter and Andreas had an open wound over his left eye.

"Come on, Peter. Help me get him to the hospital!" Peter drove, and Günter cradled his son in his arms in the passenger seat. A doctor at the hospital stitched the wound, and they were back at the Wetzels' within an hour.

The two friends relaxed in the kitchen and had a drink. Günter finally had a chance to ask Peter the question that had been on his mind for so long.

"Was that our balloon that was found near Lobenstein?" Peter had been expecting the question and was prepared to tell Günter all the details of the story. He explained what had happened and described the sudden descent into the high trees. "But, in spite of the outcome, it was a good flight. You wouldn't have believed how easy the start was, and how smooth the flight was! If you had been navigating, Günter, we would have made it. I'm sure that with your help, we would have made it. . . ."

Günter concentrated on Peter's words. "And now? What are you going to do now?"

Peter continued his story and told him what he had done in East Berlin. Günter listened and then came to the obvious conclusion. "So you're going to build another balloon. There's no other way."

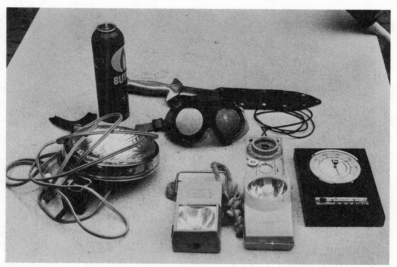

Balloon accessories: Halogen lamp, fire extinguisher, knife, goggles, flashlight, compass, altimeter. Some of the materials were found in the gondola of the second balloon, but the police were never able to trace them to the Strelzyk family.

Peter began to pressure Günter. "But we can't do it alone, Günter. We need your help. Let's build a larger balloon this time so that all eight of us can fly to the West."

Günter poured another drink for each of them. After a short pause, he said, "Give me some time to think about it, Peter. I'll get in touch with you."

A week later the two of them met again to work on their cars together. They had arranged the tools and parked the cars in front of the garage. Günter installed an automatic trailer coupler on Peter's Wartburg coupe, while Peter welded a new floor plate to the rust-eaten boot of Günter's twenty-year-old Wartburg convertible.

The men worked silently side by side for an hour, stopping occasionally to quench their thirst with beer and to wipe the sweat from their brows. It was a hot, sunny day with clear skies. The temperature was well over seventy degrees Fahrenheit.

Hesitantly, they started conversing as they had done when they were out on their electrical jobs together, discussing conditions in East Germany, and how their personal lives were affected by these conditions.

In retrospect, Peter says, "Once you've made serious plans to escape, you only see the negative side of things. All your criticism builds up until there's nothing positive left. At that point, I'm sure I thought life in East Germany was much worse than it was in reality. That day I was outraged about a new law which became effective on August 1, 1979. Its only purpose was to discourage criticism of the system. It wasn't enough for them to imprison us behind walls and barbed wire. Now they were putting muzzles on our mouths as well."

The new legislation Peter was concerned about was a reform of chapter 2 of the penal code, "Crimes Against the German Democratic Republic". Paragraph 98 of this chapter, which had formerly been headed "Collection of Intelligence", was renamed "Treasonable Transmission of Intelligence". This was the one under which Ruldolf Bahro and other critics had been sentenced. Other changes affecting individual citizens were made in paragraphs 106, 219, and

220. These paragraphs now provided drastic punishment for "subversive agitation, illegal association, and public criticism". Anyone making anti-Socialist remarks against the "social conditions, representatives, or other citizens of the German Democratic Republic on the grounds of their official or social activities" faced sentences of eight years' imprisonment. In other words, every criticism of the ruling powers within the German Democratic Republic was banned as of August 1, 1979.

Peter told Günter that, for himself at least, this was just one more reason to flee East Germany. He refused to live in a country where Socialist speeches praised the "most humane state in German history" and these same speechmakers were passing laws repressing human rights.

Günter quoted East German writer Stefan Heym, whom he had seen on West German television recently: "The people of the German Democratic Republic will be silenced. But this silence will speak louder than the most outspoken critics."

Günter added, "All this propaganda about a better standard of living is nonsense. Everyone knows that things have got worse instead of better in the last few years. And they say that prices are expected to escalate even more after the thirtieth anniversary celebration."

Peter continued his angry tirade: "Here it is thirty years after the war and the Russians are still living off us. The East German economy is like a giant cow. We feed her, while the Russians milk her and get to keep the milk. I don't consider myself a nationalist. But it hurts me to see how the German culture, and the word *German* itself, is being destroyed. Children don't even learn folk songs at school any more. And the word *German* is being crossed out of the names of organizations and clubs."

In conclusion, Peter told Günter a story he had heard about a despondent man in the local town of Schöllingroda: "The Chairman of the District Assembly shot himself! He was a victim of the overfulfilment insanity that reigns in our country. It was part of his job to send up-to-the-minute performance reports to East Berlin. Worried about the reac-

tion in the capital if he reported the true state of affairs in
Schöllingroda, this man sent a report to his superiors stating
that the harvest had been completed ahead of schedule and
that there wasn't a single potato left in the ground. Berlin
was so impressed that officials decided to honour the town
with their presence and offer congratulations in person.
When the chairman heard that the high officials were coming to visit, he realized that he had been caught in a lie and
shot himself in despair."

Günter continued to work and listen in silence while Peter
was talking. At last, Peter removed his welding glasses,
turned to Günter, and asked, "Well, Günter, what's your
answer? Are you going to help us get out of here? If we wait
too much longer, the secret police will get us first."

"I was just thinking the same thing." Günter paused and
then he said, "Don't bother to finish the welding, Peter. I
won't be needing the car much longer after all. . . ."

That evening Günter sat down with his wife Petra and
said, "I have something important to discuss with you. . . ."

"I wasn't too surprised that Günter had changed his mind
again. And this time, I had nothing against it," says Petra. "I
was so angry at the State that the sooner I could leave, the
better."

Three times Petra had applied for travel visas to West
Germany. The first time she had wanted to attend her step-
father's funeral in Frankfurt. The second time she had an
invitation to her stepbrother's wedding. Both times she was
refused. Then she received a letter from relatives in the West
informing her that her foster-mother was seriously ill. Once
again she went to the visa division of the People's Police in
Pössneck to explain the situation: "My foster-mother moved
in with relatives near Fürth several years ago when she retired. She's very ill and probably hasn't long to live. I grew
up with her and she was like a real mother to me. She did so
much for me when I was a child, even gave me the house I
live in as a wedding present. She needs me now, and I have
to go to her. I'm sure you understand. Please give me per-
mission to visit her for a few days."

Today Petra says, "I hated having to beg like that but they

were impossible to reason with. They insisted that travel visas were only issued for visits to blood relatives and told me not to act as if it were the end of the world. I was so frustrated that I wanted to throw something at the man behind that desk."

So this time, when Günter told Petra that he wanted to help Peter build another balloon, large enough to carry all eight of them, Petra was supportive. "Let me know what I can do to help. I'm with you all the way."

Günter had a pressing reason for wanting to leave the country as quickly as possible. As the "main provider" for his family, one who was also contributing to the State by renovating his home, Günter's mandatory military service had been postponed. But his time had run out, and he had received an induction notice in July ordering him to report to a Pioneer Unit on November 1. Since draft evasion is subject to severe punishment in East Germany, Günter opted to leave as soon as he could. On August 13, Günter called in sick to the personnel department of People's Owned Trucking and Transport in Saalfeld. Two weeks later, on August 27, he called in again to tell them that he was taking his holiday.

On Saturday, July 27, the day that the two men had worked on their cars together, they sat down at the Strelzyks' kitchen table and outlined new plans for the construction of another, even larger, hot-air balloon. This balloon would have to be able to carry a total weight of three-quarters of a ton. They calculated that at a temperature of 212 degrees Fahrenheit, the balloon would have to hold 5,200 cubic yards of air. This meant that the balloon would be over 21 yards wide and 28 yards long, comparable to the size of an eight-storey house. It wasn't until much later that Günter Wetzel and Peter Strelzyk realized that, there in Peter's kitchen, they had started on the largest hot-air balloon in the history of Europe.

From the very first stage, the third balloon proved to be much more difficult to build than the previous two. Peter and Günter had to assume that since balloon number two had been discovered on the border, all textile stores in East

Germany would be on the lookout for anyone wanting to buy more than a few feet of airtight material. And the balloon builders calculated that they would need 1,430 square yards!

In the next few weeks they drove more than 2,500 miles back and forth to twenty-seven cities throughout the Republic trying to buy nylon fabric, taffeta, and mattress ticking. They pooled their savings accounts and even contributed money they had set aside for their children. In all, they spent more than ten thousand marks for the fabric alone.

"We were still scared," admits Doris. "Every time we walked into a store we expected someone to grab us and hold us until the police arrived." Günter went with them on the first few trips but, as soon as he had enough material to work with, he stayed behind in the Strelzyks' cellar at his old sewing machine.

The women sometimes shopped alone for mattress ticking because it aroused less suspicion than when the men asked for it. Later, Peter and Günter took turns pretending that they needed material for sails for a sailing club in Gera or tents for a camping club in Saalfeld.

To their surprise almost no one seemed suspicious of them. Only once, in Jena, did Peter panic and leave a department store: the head of the department asked once too often why he needed so much material. Then he went behind a glass wall and made a telephone call. He returned and told Peter that it would take fifteen or twenty minutes to get the material from the stock room. When the man left to get the material, Peter sneaked out of the store, jumped in the car, and drove away.

Günter, who knew his way around the cities of Rostock, Stralsund, Schwerin, and Magdeburg, left his sewing machine to go with Peter to the northern part of the country. But in these larger towns, they were seldom able to find the quality they needed for the balloon. Surprisingly enough, there was more available in the provinces.

So they drove to the cities and towns of Calau and Cottbus, Triptis and Zeulenroda. In the famous trading centre of Leipzig they bought twenty yards of nylon silk, in Weimar, where the German constitution had been signed after World War I, sixty-six yards of mattress ticking, in Gehren sixty-five yards, in Ilmenau one hundred, and in Halle they even bought 165 yards. "We gained more confidence and dared to buy larger quantities each time."

By the beginning of August, they had covered most of East Germany and had acquired material in all the colours of the rainbow. Günter drew up an interim balance and found that they had 837 square yards, just about half of what they needed.

There were many days when Peter, Petra, and Doris came back empty-handed. In vain they went to three stores in Leipzig. They left the towns of Eilenburg, Torgau, and Finsterwalde without even a foot of fabric to show for their efforts.

On August 14, Peter arrived home tired and irritable. Doris had been waiting for him nervously. He reached for the newspaper that was always on the kitchen table, and Doris said, "I hid it in the living room so that the children wouldn't see it. Look at page 2. . . ."

Peter stomped to the living room and got the *Volkswacht* from the shelf in the cupboard. He glanced at the headline on the front page: "Russian: Language of Cooperation toward Freedom." Page 2 began with a long article describing an exhibition titled *Steps into Space*. Below that, Peter found the article that had upset Doris. There was a small photograph of several very familar objects: a barometer, a pocket watch, some goggles, and a pair of pliers. Under the photo was printed: "The People's Police ask you to help!"

Peter read the article: "The People's Police reports: these articles were left at the scene of a serious crime. . . . The barometer pictured above is gold-plated and has three holes drilled in the upper edge of the casing. The pocket watch is an old model manufactured by UMF in Ruhla; it has no jewels. Who can offer information about the person or persons who owned these objects? If requested, information leading to the whereabouts of this or these persons will be kept confidential. Please direct information to the Gera People's Police, Criminal Division telephone 61-73-19, or to any local People's Police station."

Peter's hands shook uncontrollably as he put the paper down on the kitchen table. "Well, now they really *are* hunting us." That was his only comment.

He noticed that the report didn't mention the balloon and gave no indication that the "serious crime" was an attempt to flee the Republic. "The Vopos and the Stasi know that the population isn't likely to help in cases of border violation. So they have to be vague about the nature of the crime."

Peter showed the paper to Günter who, pausing typically as if collecting his thoughts, said, "Peter, this isn't such bad news after all. It means that they haven't found anything substantial yet. They're feeling their way in the dark. They have no evidence. The things in that picture can be found in almost every household in the GDR. They won't get far with that, that's for sure." Günter poured two glasses of schnapps to calm their nerves. "It's just a question of who's faster, them or us." And Günter went back to work at the sewing machine in the Strelzyks' cellar. From then on, he worked twenty hours a day.

Peter's thirty-seventh birthday was on August 15. But he had no inclination to celebrate. He spent the day welding the thin platform that would be the floor of the gondola. Toward midnight he drank a glass of Spanish red wine with his wife at home. Doris had bought the bottle at the Pössneck delicatessen for twenty-two marks. But Peter was too preoccupied to enjoy it. Day after day he scanned the pages of the local paper looking for new information about the search.

News of the day on August 15 as presented in the *Volkswacht*: an article headlined "Teddy's Spirit" called Pössneck workers together in memory of Ernst Thälmann. "Collectives are requested to assemble at Ethel & Julius Rosenberg Platz and at the Ernst Thälmann memorial on Neustädter Street." First Magdeburg team stormer, Joachim Streich, was chosen best German soccer player of the year. The column "Where to Go Today" advertised the East German film *You Will Not Find Peace* at the Central Theatre on Breiten Street (Pössneck's only movie theatre).

At about three o'clock the next afternoon, the balloon builders' work was interrupted by an ear-shattering noise outside. Günter was so startled that he lost the thread in the machine. Peter stopped working on the burner system and ran out to the yard where Doris was hanging out washing.

"There's a helicopter flying right over the house!" yelled Doris to Peter when she saw him standing in the doorway. It was true. A helicopter with the emblem of the National People's Army was flying so low over the Strelzyks' yard that the wind of the propellers knocked the apples off the trees.

The frightened balloon builders watched from behind the curtains as the helicopter circled the house four times. Doris says, "I was sure that they were going to land in the yard and that armed soldiers would storm the house and capture us." But the helicopter disappeared as quickly as it had come, circling the Pössneck marketplace before finally turning north toward the foothills of the Thuringian Forest.

"We thought that they had got a tip from someone in the neighbourhood who had read the newspaper article and that they wanted to check out the house from the air before coming to pick us up. It wasn't until several days later that we found out what had really happened. A soldier had run away from the Soviet barracks near Saalfeld. That's who they had been looking for. They found him too, three or four days later. I guess he couldn't make it over the border. We heard that he got lost somewhere near the death zone."

Another strange story circulated in Pössneck at about the same time, about a man who had been apprehended in the neighbouring town of Saalfeld. Rumour had it that he had built a kite and the police had caught him on Wetzstein, a 2,600-foot mountain on the border between Thuringia and Franconia, while he was waiting for a favourable wind to take him to West Germany. "Some people came up with the damnedest schemes to get out of the country before the anniversary celebration." Günter grinned as he related the story.

Peter and the two women resumed their shopping expeditions. Again they travelled to Erfurt, Arnstadt, Gotha, Meissen, Jena, and Weimar. They came home with bits and pieces of material from everywhere they went. On September 1, they bought the last thirty yards of red mattress ticking in a department store in Jena, bringing them to a grand total of 1,500 square yards.

Günter had been busy cutting the material into triangles

and sewing it together as they brought it home. It was tedious, repetitive work. He would sew an 18.5-yard triangular piece to a 7.5-yard straight piece, and sew that to a 12-yard piece which formed a point at the top. Günter used enough thread to stretch nearly two miles.

In the meantime Peter had finished the second burner system, using the same method he had developed for the second balloon. This time, however, the valve opening was twice as large, .16 inch instead of .08 inch. He calculated that the flame would shoot to 46 feet inside the 82-foot balloon. The gondola and platform were ready too. The floor, which was to support eight people, was made of laminated steel, only .031 inch thick. To give the thin steel more stability, Peter had welded underneath in the corners and diagonally.

When Petra walked into the laundry room and saw the finished gondola and the steel floor for the first time, she was taken aback. "It'll never hold all eight of us," she thought. She was reminded of the disaster nightmare that had haunted her for the last few weeks. Later all four balloon builders admitted that they had been plagued by bad dreams at night.

Peter says, "I would wake up in the morning trembling and bathed in perspiration. I would dream that the platform broke and I stood there grabbing on to a corner of the gondola with one hand and holding a child with the other. The other child tumbled through the hole in the gondola floor. I never knew if it was Andreas or Frank. Or I would dream that the balloon caught fire, shot up thousands of feet in the air, fell apart, and dropped to the ground."

Doris had similar nightmares. "But once I dreamt that everything went according to plan and that we landed safely. After we landed, cars drove up to us. People got out and applauded and put their arms around us."

Peter, who had designed the gondola, wanted to convince the rest of the passengers that the platform would be able to handle a heavy load. So he set up a test in the laundry room in the cellar, putting bricks under the four corners of the structure so that the thin floor was suspended in midair. He told everyone to get in. The four adults and four children stood on the platform and jumped around, pleased to find that although the platform vibrated, it held together.

At the same time, they also experimented with positioning themselves for the trip on the 4-foot-6-inch by 4-foot-6-inch space. The adults stood with their backs to the corner posts and the children were posted between their parents with the four propane bottles in the middle. All eight of them had enough room to stand in the tiny gondola and all of them were able to hold on to something for support.

The shell of the balloon was finished and seemed to be perfect. The burner system had been tested and found to be in working order. By September 14, the third balloon, 28 yards by 22 yards, the largest they had built, was finally ready to take them across the border.

Each of the passengers prepared for the secret departure in his or her own way.

Frank, expecting to be far away by then, signed up for a soccer game with school friends for the next week. "I knew that they would be suspicious if I said that I didn't want to play."

His mother, Doris, continued to work at the Pössneck Savings Bank. "I knew that my co-workers would have to pick up the pieces when I left, but I started new projects anyway."

Petra, quality control technician at People's Owned Tool Factory, signed up for a two-week holiday beginning immediately. "Some of my colleagues noticed that I seemed more serious than usual when I said goodbye that day. One commented that I seemed so sad."

The day before they hoped to leave, Günter put new hubcaps on his old Wartburg, making sure that the neighbours saw him. "I didn't want anyone to suspect anything, now that we were so close to the big day. It occurred to me while I was working on the car that soon it would become State property."

14

"Up, Up, and Away!"

They had only to wait for favourable weather conditions—a cloudless sky and a steady wind to the west. To their disappointment, Saturday, September 15, was cloudy, warm, and humid, with almost no wind at all.

"We had just about given up hope," says Peter. "But in the late afternoon a cold front came in from the north and there was a heavy thunderstorm. And by late evening the clouds were gone and there was a steady wind."

Günter and Peter listened to the weather forecasts on television and radio as they had done so often before. They said it was going to remain cold and clear. Günter switched to Bavaria Channel III to get the detailed report for gliders, which gave wind direction and velocity at various altitudes. But on that particular day, the announcer broke into uncontrollable laughter just as she came on the air. "She never did stop laughing long enough to give the forecast," remembers Günter. "We were furious when another announcer came on and apologized for his colleague. All he said was 'and now back to music' and we sat there with no information at all about the wind. . . ."

So shortly before midnight the two balloonists drove to

the heights above the town to test the wind direction and velocity. Conditions were perfect. The wind was blowing toward the west, toward the Federal Republic of Germany.

Their families were ready to go when the men returned to the house. "We didn't pack anything so that there wouldn't be too much weight in the balloon," says Doris. "And we had agreed to leave everything at home."

The trailer with the gondola and balloon was already attached to the blue-and-white Wartburg. There wasn't enough room for all eight people in the cramped Wartburg so Günter and Frank went ahead on a moped shortly after midnight. Peter, the two women, and the three smaller children followed in the crowded car. The car was so weighed down that the springs touched the axles and they were only able to travel at twenty-four miles per hour on the winding road.

In Ziegenrück, a People's Police car passed them. Peter held his breath in fear until they saw the officials stop the car and go into a nearby inn, apparently to spotcheck the Free German Youth dance which took place there every Saturday night.

They reached Oberlemnitz shortly before one o'clock and turned off onto a sandy path to a clearing in the woods, not far from the place where the Strelzyks had taken off alone on July 4. Although the place was between Heinersdorf and Oberlemnitz, only about eighteen miles from Pössneck, it had taken the fugitives nearly forty-five minutes to get there in the slow, overloaded Wartburg. By that time, Günter and Frank had already checked out the area.

From the clearing, which was situated on a hill above the railroad tracks from Lobenstein to Saalfeld, they had a panoramic view of Thuringia below. Several miles away, a few lights were still visible in farmhouses where people were celebrating the harvest.

It was chilly, just a few degrees above freezing. Petra opened a bottle of currant wine to warm them and poured glasses for the two men and Frank.

At 1:30 A.M. they started setting up the equipment. First they spread the balloon out on the damp ground. Then Günter and Peter lifted the gondola from the trailer and placed it in front of the balloon. They hammered four 3-foot-long iron pins into the soft ground and stretched nylon lines from the corner supports of the gondola to the pins. Three nylon lines also connected the gondola to the balloon neck. Peter and Frank wired the cold air blower to the fourteen-horsepower motorcycle motor.

The flashlights flickered eerily in the clearing and the moon rose above the treetops, giving them more light by which to work. Petra busied herself in the background with the smaller children, eleven-year-old Andreas Strelzyk and her own sons, five-year-old Peter and two-year-old Andreas. Andreas kept pulling away and running excitedly back and forth between the men. The tranquillizers they'd given him seemed to have had no effect. Petra finally had to grab his hand to keep him from getting in the way.

2:00 A.M. They were ready to go. The flight from East to West Germany was about to begin. They could not know that they were about to face near catastrophe. But later, when the flight was behind them, they would agree that they must have had a whole squadron of guardian angels accompanying them.

Peter signalled Frank to fill the small motorcycle tank with gasoline. Then he started the 250 cubic centimetre machine which roared loudly, in spite of the built-in muffler. A freight train rattled by below the clearing, drowning the noise of the motor, but they were so obsessed with the preparations that they didn't hear it until it had passed them.

No one seemed to hear them. Slowly the blower pushed air into the limp balloon and it began to fill. Günter stood in the gondola with his hands above his head trying to hold the sides of the balloon apart so that the air could push through to the top. Frank and Doris held the neck of the balloon open from the bottom. Petra held her son Andreas in her arms and kept the other two children near her. Within ten minutes the balloon was half-full. Peter called to Günter to get out.

2:10 A.M. Frank lit a match to the butane burner and handed it to his father. Peter used this tiny burner to ignite the torch. It hissed as the flame shot out of the pipe. Peter directed the flame into the balloon neck, which was now being held open by Frank and Günter. Then he turned the valve all the way and a long pointed flame shot forward. Peter felt tremendous heat on his face. His eyes watered and he was blinded by the light. He smelled burning hair and realized that he had singed his hair and clothes. The flame was pushed backward several times because the cold air in the balloon still offered too much resistance. But Frank and Günter were just able to jump aside in time to avoid being burned. Then they resumed their positions at the neck of the balloon. The air began to get warm, the uptake increased, and finally the long flame was sucked into the balloon.

2:15 A.M. To increase the air pressure still more, Günter took the cold air blower and stood behind Peter, who was still holding the torch in position. The propeller pushed the hot air into the balloon at 3,000 rpm.

2:16 A.M. The balloon finally lifted from the ground. Petra, who was standing about twenty yards away, describes what she saw: "It was beautiful! It must have been as high as a church steeple. All those bright stripes looked fantastic, like modern art." Her son Peter asked excitedly, "Mommy, Mommy, is the balloon going to take us to the sky?"

2:17 A.M. Günter ignited the burner, which was mounted between the four propane bottles in the gondola. They had learned from previous tests that when they changed over from torch to burner, the balloon lost air and shrank, so Peter continued to direct the heat of the torch into the balloon for another twenty or thirty seconds. The two friends stood shoulder to shoulder in the gondola while their wives and children watched wide-eyed from the edge of the clearing. The lines from the gondola to the balloon and those from the ground to the gondola were stretched as taut as they could be, putting tremendous stress on the anchoring system.

Günter called to the women, "Hurry, get in! We're ready to go!"

Frank and his mother were the first to climb over the guardrail, followed by Andreas and Peter. Petra lifted little Andreas over the line and was the last to board the gondola.

Peter extinguished the torch and threw it overboard to the ground.

2:20 A.M. "Cut the lines!" ordered Peter. Frank and Günter tried simultaneously to cut all four lines connecting the gondola to the anchor pegs in the ground. But somehow they only managed to cut two lines at first. Suddenly one of the heavy iron pegs catapulted out of the ground and caught Frank and his brother Andreas on the head in its flight. Blood ran down the children's faces but in the excitement that ensued, no one noticed it. . . .

For the gondola now hung at an angle of forty-five degrees by only one line. The passengers slid sideward. Fortunately the propane bottles were mounted securely on a rack, or they would have fallen over on the passengers.

2:22 A.M. With the gondola tilted as it was, the burner flame was dangerously close to the fabric shell of the balloon. Suddenly the material was in flames and the fire threatened to spread to the top of the balloon! Günter grabbed the fire extinguisher and the fluid hissed toward the flame. Within a few seconds the fire was out. But Peter knew how close they had come to disaster. "A few seconds longer and the fire would have raised the temperature in the balloon enough to pull the last anchor line loose. We would have shot up in the air and then dropped like a rock to the ground. We were very fortunate."

2:24 A.M. Günter cut the last line with a diver's knife. The gondola shook unsteadily until the platform gradually regained a horizontal position while the balloon slowly lifted from the ground. The long burner flame pointed straight up again, a safe distance away from the walls of the balloon. They were out of danger. The balloon climbed at a speed of 650 to 780 feet per minute. Frank glanced at his watch. "Within two minutes, we were already so high that I couldn't see anything on the ground. It was very dark. All I could make out was the contrast between the woods and the fields."

No one panicked. No one even seemed terribly excited. Everyone was too busy. Peter had both hands full trying to hold the burner straight up. Günter watched the altimeter and the two women took care of the children.

They stood in the gondola just as they had practised in the cellar. The four adults held on to the four iron poles in the corners facing the burner flame, while the children stood between them and the propane bottles. Petra held two-year-old Andreas by both hands and caught him between her knees so that he couldn't run around.

2:27 A.M. The bright red light of the burner flame fell on the faces of the fleeing balloonists. Doris glanced at Frank, standing next to her, and was shocked. His face was pallid and he was bleeding from a wound over his left eye. "My God! What happened to you?" Frank looked at her questioningly. "I had felt something hit me but everything happened so fast that I guess I didn't have time to notice any pain. I didn't even realize that I was bleeding until my mother called my attention to it. But it didn't really hurt." Eleven-year-old Andreas was bleeding too. It was then that they discovered that they had forgotten the first-aid kit, which was still in the boot of the Wartburg, so they wiped the blood away with their jacket sleeves.

2:23 A.M. It was absolutely quiet for several minutes. No one said a word. They were alone in the sky with the stars. Fortunately there were no clouds to worry about this time. Peter kept his eyes on the flame and Günter watched the altimeter. "Only eight minutes after takeoff we were already at 6,560 feet." Peter lowered the flame to hold this altitude. They were travelling at an approximate speed of twenty-five to thirty knots, about thirty miles an hour.

Suddenly Günter yelled, "Damn! Look down there! There are spotlights below us and it looks as if they're searching for us."

2:36 A.M. They calculated that the balloon was now about a mile above the border, somewhere between Lobenstein and Blankenstein. They knew that a border troop of the People's Army was stationed down there and that the halogen lights installed in the watchtowers were powerful enough to illuminate the three-mile border strip on the ground.

The beams swung menacingly across the sky as if they had spotted something, lost it, and were trying to find it again. Frank saw several beams of light meet in the sky and

The air in the balloon was heated with a homemade blowtorch fashioned from a stovepipe and attached to four bottles of propane gas.

thought that it looked like a big crooked finger pointing at them.

Petra says, "Suddenly it was brighter than it had been in the gondola. I didn't know what it was until I heard the men shouting about searchlights."

Peter opened the valve of the burner and the balloon surged upward, out of the range of the spotlights. The altimeter registered 8,500 as they left the lights below them and behind them. They were out of danger.

"I still don't know what we would have done if they had spotted us," says Peter. "I do know that there are no antiaircraft weapons on that part of the border. As far as I knew, they only had machine guns and we were high enough to be out of their range."

2:38 A.M. A group of lights appeared ahead of them. The balloon swayed peacefully about two to three miles away from the Hirschberg Autobahn which is illuminated at night. The navigator, Günter, was pleased. "I knew that we were on course. We just had to hope that the wind wouldn't die down."

2:42 A.M. Little Andreas was restless and cold. His mother says, "He wouldn't stop squirming and he kept crying, 'Mommy, Mommy, Mommy.' I squatted down and tried to calm him with a lullaby:

> From toyland comes a teddy bear,
> Soft, and warm, and sweet;
> All the children beckon him . . .

I forgot the rest of the words. I'd sung the song a hundred times, but suddenly I couldn't remember the rest of the words! I don't think that it was fear that made me forget. . . . But Andreas was calmer already anyway."

2:45 A.M. The flame seemed to be burning unevenly and Peter opened the valve all the way. But it continued to flicker. He asked, "How high are we now?"

"Still over 6,500 feet, but we're descending!"

2:46 A.M. The propane flame got smaller. First it flickered and then small, sharp flames started flickering around the burner pipe, making little explosions. First they thought that the pipe was clogged but then they realized that, improbable as it seemed, they were running out of fuel. They had only been in the air for twenty-three minutes and they had calculated that, with propane being released in equal amounts from the four bottles, they would have fuel for at least thirty to thirty-five minutes. But they were wrong.

Günter tried to start the large propane burner again with matches. Ironically, the brand name of the matches was Freie Welt (Free World). But the burner was out—and the balloon continued its descent.

2:48 A.M. Colourful lights emerged below them. Doris watched a traffic light change from red to yellow to green as it got closer and closer.

2:50 A.M. Günter was finally able to relight the burner using a whole handful of matches. Once again the flame shot up into the balloon—only for a few seconds, but long enough for the lights below them to disappear in the distance. Then it was dark again in the gondola, as well as on the ground.

The balloon turned slowly as they lost steering power. The flame flickered for the last time as the last drop of propane burned away. They had used nearly one hundred pounds of propane. The air in the balloon began to cool. It sank faster. The earth came closer into view and the frightened passengers stared into the unknown darkness. Slowly, details on the ground came into view and they could see hills and houses, clumps of trees, and individual farmsteads. Everything was still blurred and ghostly.

Günter shone his battery-powered halogen lamp on the ground. Now they wanted to draw attention to themselves, no matter which side of the border they were on. A crash landing seemed inevitable and, if one of them should be injured, they would probably need immediate help. It would be best to have someone find them as quickly as possible, even it it had to be the East German police.

2:52 A.M. At one hundred feet, the halogen lamp picked out the outline of the treetops in the forest below. Then the light fell on bushes, and then on the ground. The balloon swayed over a clump of pine trees, bent a thin acacia tree, sideswiped a few branches, and landed with a thud on the grassy ground a scant 550 feet from a high-voltage electrical line. The gondola rocked back and forth when it hit the ground and dragged several yards before coming to a complete stop. The passengers held on to the corner posts. The balloon itself caught in the treetops and pulled the gondola up on one side, almost overturning the propane bottles. Günter cut the lines connecting the gondola to the balloon. No one, not even the frightened children, panicked.

3:52 A.M. The flight of the two families from Thuringia was over. It had lasted twenty-eight minutes.

One by one, the passengers climbed out of the gondola, women and children first. No one seemed to have suffered more than a few scratches and bruises.

Doris was the first to ask, "Are we in the West?" But no one knew the answer.

Peter ordered the women and children to find a place to hide while he and Günter went to look around and try to get their bearings.

"Where are we going, Mommy?" asked five-year-old Peter.

"Come, child, let's follow the moon . . . ," answered Petra.

The sky was still clear and there was a thin sliver of moon. The women took cover under a large hedge separating two harvested wheatfields. From there, they could see a street light about three hundred feet away, illuminating a narrow strip of asphalt road.

In the meantime, the two men had reached a large wooden barn. The door was open and they went in. They saw a modern tractor and in the beam of Peter's flashlight they read the owner's name painted on the side.

"This seems to be privately owned. We don't have private farmers in the East any more."

Günter agreed and added, "They looked like pretty small fields from the air too. The collectives at home are much larger."

A few seconds later they heard the sound of a motor as a truck drove by on the narrow road. But the two men couldn't tell in the dark whether it was a Mercedes or a Skoda. More time passed. Then a passenger car approached.

Günter thought that it sounded like a Moskwitsch, but then he saw that it had square headlights.

The car stopped only a few yards from the barn on the slightly raised road. They saw two men in the front seat. Finally, Günter was able to identify the make of car—an Audi 80. One word was written on the side of the car in luminous letters—*Police*.

"My God, Peter," whispered Günter. "We've done it! They're West Germans!"

An artist's rendering of the takeoff preparations on September 16, 1979. The wind was blowing to the west.

Finkenflug, the place where the balloon came down. Residents of the valley area reported the presence of a low-flying object, one that had a mysterious, eerie glow.

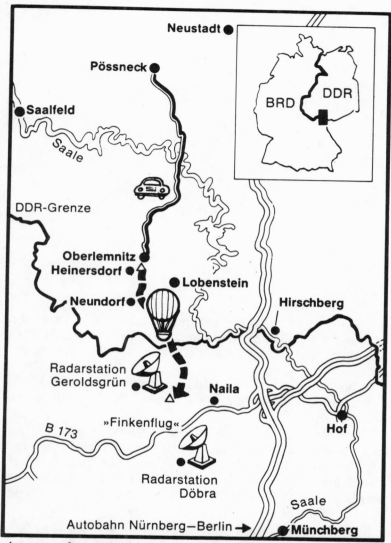

A map outlining the path of the balloon flight on September 16, 1979. The families drove from Pössneck to Oberlemnitz, where they prepared the balloon for takeoff, and landed in "Finkenflug" near the West German town of Naila.

15

Where Are We?

The balloonists had landed in a region known as Finkenflug, a suburb of the little town of Naila in Upper Franconia. Less than three hours had gone by since they left Pössneck for the last time.

Although Pössneck and Naila are only thirty miles apart, they lie in very different worlds—one in the East, the other in the West.

The road connecting the two towns has been closed for thirty years and a death strip with barbed wire, automatic trip wires, and minefields separates the 20,000 inhabitants of Pössneck from the 9,400 inhabitants of Naila. But on the morning of Sunday, September 16, natives of Pössneck and Naila crossed paths in a very unusual way.

Naila, 2:40 A.M. It was dark in the small town in the Franconian Forest. The last revellers had long since stumbled out of the Froschgrün Inn and gone home to bed. The only lights were those in the hospital and police station in the marketplace. One car cruised up and down the quiet streets, a green-and-white Audi 80 with luminous lettering on the side—*Police*—radio code Saale 13-3.

Patrolman Rudolf Gölkel was at the wheel and his friend

and colleague Captain Walter Hamann sat beside him in the passenger seat. Rudi and Walter had been working together for many years to maintain law and order in Naila. Walter Hamann, a cheerful, good-natured man who usually kept his pistol tucked away under his belt, looked upon his job as a hobby. "The two of us do everything here. We direct traffic and catch criminals. It's more fun than work."

The week before, there had been a serious automobile accident in Naila and three days later the two policemen had even caught a burglar red-handed. On this particular day, they had started work at 6:30 P.M. and had spent hours tracking down a hit-and-run driver who had damaged three parked cars. They found the light brown Ford Camaro and impounded it. Nothing else unusual had taken place in Naila that day.

Now, at 2:40 A.M., as car 13-3 cruised past the Naila High School, Patrolman Gölkel saw a strange, extraterrestrial sight a mile away. At first he thought that a house was on fire, but his companion grabbed a pair of binoculars and said, "No, it can't be a house because it's up in the sky. It looks like a burning triangle, a kite or something. . . ."

Slowly and noiselessly the flaming unidentified object hovered toward Naila. The two policemen stared at the sky for several minutes before turning the car around and driving to the army barracks on Frankenwald Street. They reported the strange flying object and suggested that army personnel call the radar station in the neighbouring town of Döbraberg to find out if they had spotted anything on their screen.

The answer was negative. Nothing had been seen on the screen in the 2,600-foot observation tower which overlooked the German border.

"Maybe I was imagining things," thought Captain Hamann as he shook his head and told two army officers to go outside and look up in the sky in a northwesterly direction. But there, where the bright triangle had been a few minutes before, was now nothing but stars.

"Now *they* thought I was imagining things too," remembers Captain Hamann.

They weren't the only ones on that morning, shortly before 3:00 A.M., who thought that they were seeing things.
Bank clerk Dieter Künzel and his wife Evelyn were returning home with friends from the neighbouring town of Hof,
where they had spent the night dancing in the Silberspindel
Night Club. Dieter had been drinking beer all evening, so
his wife drove their green Lancia back to Naila.

Just as they passed an ice-cream parlour on the edge of
town, Dieter said casually, "Look at that big red star up
there in the sky." His wife and friends in the back seat saw
the object, too, and wondered why it disappeared and reap-
peared again.

The Künzels dropped their friends off at their apartment
and continued on to their bungalow on Albin Klöber Street.
They saw the strange light again as they walked from the
car to the house. It was coming closer and getting larger.
Evelyn, a young, intelligent woman, became more and more
concerned as the flickering light neared.

"I had always thought that stories about life on other
planets were nonsense, but now I was beginning to wonder.
Scenes from *Invasion of the Body Snatchers* flashed through
my mind."

Quietly, almost on tiptoe, the Künzels walked across the
flagstone path to their front door. They opened the door and
turned off the porch light. Evelyn thought, "Maybe there is
other life in the universe."

Bewildered, her husband shook his head. "It can't possibly
be an aeroplane. I've never seen anything like it."

The couple went into the living room and stood in the
dark in front of the picture window with the panorama view
staring at the sky. The flickering object came closer, disap-
pearing and then reappearing again. And then they saw
beams of light pointing from the thing to the ground below.

Evelyn said, "Here they come. . . ."

Several terrifying minutes passed before the Künzels saw
the large silhouette. "First we thought it was a parachute
but then we could see that it was a giant pear-shaped balloon dropping to the ground about five hundred yards away
at a rather high speed."

No longer worried, but still very excited, Evelyn picked up the telephone and dialled 110. A man's voice answered, "Naila Police Station." Evelyn told the man what they had just seen. "A balloon has landed here. Practically in our front yard. I don't know if anyone is in it or not. Please send someone quickly!"

Patrolman Spörl, who was on the switchboard that night, had already heard from his colleagues in car 13-3 that a strange object had been seen hovering in the sky. He answered matter-of-factly, "Okay. We'll send someone to check it out." He radioed the news to patrolmen Gölkel and Hamann who immediately drove to Albin Klöber Street past the Künzels' house toward Finkenflug.

Gölkel switched on the high beams and swerved the car several times so that the light shone into the fields on both sides of the road. The two officers stopped near an old barn and stared into the dimly lit landscape.

"Suddenly two men came running toward us from the barn. That in itself was strange," jokes Hamann, "because at that time of night people usually run away when they see the police."

One of the men, still out of breath, asked, "Are we in West Germany?"

The policemen, at a loss for words, nodded their heads affirmatively. The strangers hugged them and started screaming and yelling.

"Hurrah! We made it! We did it!"

Günter pulled a red flare out of his pocket and lit it. The women and children saw the all-clear signal from their hiding place and knew that they had landed in the Federal Republic of Germany. Laughing and shouting, they rushed across the field and up the slope to their husbands and the police. Unable to control her joy, the usually proper Petra threw herself on Captain Hamann's sturdy chest. He lost his balance and the two Germans, one from the East and the other from the West, slid arm in arm down the hill.

When they'd calmed down a bit, car 13-3 called in to order a Volkswagen bus from the Naila Red Cross station to pick up the refugees. Captain Hamann says, "It was a very

Patrolman Gölkel and Captain Hamann, the first two men to reach the scene of the landing. They were joyously hugged by Peter and Günter when the two refugees learned that they were West German police. Here the two men are shown standing in the barn where Peter and Günter hid.

humourous situation. First came the two men, then the two women beside themselves with joy—and then more and more children came out of the bushes. We didn't believe them at first when they said that they had all come in a balloon."

To prove it, and because she remembered that she had left something there, Petra dragged the police captain to the landing place. She asked him to shine his flashlight on the gondola until she found a package carefully wrapped in brown paper. She picked up the package, walked back with it in her hand to the others, and unwrapped it. The package contained a bottle of Faber champagne which she had bought at the Pössneck delicatessen for 35 marks. In West Germany she could have bought the same bottle for 3.90 marks. "But that wasn't important," says Petra, beaming. "I had heard somewhere that a bottle of champagne has to be on board every balloon flight for good luck. It's tradition."

Petra found it hard to believe that they had really made it to the West. "A few minutes after we landed, it already seemed as though the flight had been a dream. And later, at the police station, the whole situation seemed so unreal. There we sat in a police station, the likes of which I had never seen before. Outside there were painted windowboxes with flowers. And inside, all those wonderful friendly policemen. Even the cell, where I rested on a cot for a few minutes, was warm and friendly looking. It was almost like a tiny hotel room, with magazines next to the cot and everything. There was a tremendous meal for us on the desk at the station—sausage, ham, and cheese sandwiches. A policeman made coffee for us and one of them even managed to find clean nappies in the middle of the night. The baby was so excited when we landed that he had had an accident. And the whole time we were there, we laughed and hugged each other."

It was 4:00 A.M. when the East German champagne cork hit the ceiling of the West German police station and the Wetzels and Strelzyks drank a toast to the success of their balloon flight.

"Günter had to pinch me to convince me that I wasn't

dreaming," says Petra. "He pinched me so hard that I screamed, but at least I knew it was true. We really were in the West!"

It was beginning to get light outside by the time Captain Hamann telephoned his report to Robert Strobel, Mayor of Naila: "Mr. Mayor, several refugees from Pössneck landed here in a balloon tonight."

The mayor, still half-asleep, answered, "Come on, Captain Hamann. I don't like jokes in the middle of the night. Especially if they're not even funny. . . ."

16

"The Wonder of Naila"

Captain Hamann had to repeat his story over the telephone several times, insisting that it was true. But there was so much laughter and celebration in the background that Naila's mayor didn't believe the story until Police Director Oster, from Hof, arrived in Naila and informed the mayor in person. Finally the thirty-nine-year-old mayor, a member of the Christian Socialist Union Party, climbed out of bed and hurried to the police station to see the "wonder of Naila", as it was already being called.

Mayor Strobel wasn't the only one who found the story hard to believe. Reinhard Beck, honorary leader of the Bavarian Red Cross unit in Naila, was a man familiar with unusual situations and disasters. But the thirty-five-year-old man thought that "the whole story was a dumb game thought up by one of my men". At a party the previous Tuesday, the leader of Reinhard's column had tipped him off that there would probably be an emergency drill that weekend. "But when nothing had happened by Saturday night, I assumed that they had changed their minds."

On Sunday morning, shortly after 3 A.M., his men came to drag him out of bed. "We've had a call from the police. A balloon with eight East German refugees has landed in a meadow in Finkenflug. There are children among them."

Reinhard was disappointed that they hadn't been able to think of anything more original than a balloon landing—the previous drill had been a private plane crash. Just to be sure, he called the police station.

"Is this a drill?"

"Get going, it's the real thing!"

Reinhard alerted the rest of his people and a Volkswagen bus with a large red cross painted on the side arrived in Finkenflug at 3:36 A.M., about thirty minutes after the landing.

"Everything was in terrible confusion. There were men and women and children dancing around the two policemen, hugging each other and patting each other on the back. It was the funniest emergency I had ever seen."

It wasn't until someone pointed to the balloon hanging in the trees a few hundred yards away that he unwillingly accepted the fact that this was indeed a serious situation. The first thing they did was bandage the two children who had been hit with the iron peg at the beginning of the flight back in East Germany. Later the wounds were sewn up at the Naila hospital.

Reinhard Beck, a large, bearded man, was the first to organize aid for the refugees. In the middle of the night, he called Mr. Merklein, a butcher from the neighbouring town of Marlesreuth, who jumped out of bed to bring platters of sausage and ham to the Naila police station. A baker brought fresh rolls, and someone else brought beer. Eight cots were set up in the Red Cross classroom and the heat was turned up in the building.

Peter was deeply moved. "It was a fantastic welcome. Everyone was so excited that I could hardly get my thoughts together."

Günter, the quieter of the two balloonists, was excited at first but became very pensive as the night wore on. "I hugged everyone who came close to me at the barn but then, after we arrived at the police station, I felt I needed to be alone with my thoughts. I'm not a churchgoer and I had never thought much about religion, but I knew that we had been very, very lucky. We had been in danger several times: at takeoff, during the flight, and when we crash-landed. Maybe there is a higher power that was protecting us throughout our adventure."

All eight of the refugees spent the last few hours of the night at the Red Cross station. But no one slept in the narrow cots provided for them. The children were excited and irritable. Günter felt a growing pain in his left calf and was taken to the hospital at 7 A.M. The doctor said that he had torn several muscles, probably when the gondola hit the ground. They put his leg in a splint and gave him pain-killing drugs.

Günter Wetzel, who had risked his life that night to escape from East Germany, finally fell asleep in a hospital room in West Germany. Above his head on the white wall was a framed biblical quote:

> He will not suffer thy foot to be moved;
> He that keepeth thee will not slumber.
> Psalms 121:3

Instead of relaxing that day, Peter had to start down the long path of official red tape. First he was driven in a police car to the Bavarian Border Police station in Hof, where an officer was waiting for him at the entrance.

"Welcome to free Germany," he said as he shook Peter's hand. "I have to inform you that you have been accused of trespassing in air space belonging to the Federal Republic of Germany." He added immediately, "But since it was apparently the only possible way out of East Germany, I doubt if anyone will press charges." Smiling, he said, "Now, may I have your full name please?"

Instead of answering, Peter reached in his pocket and pulled out a blue passport with the East German emblem and placed it on the desk in front of him. On the cover was printed his personal identification number X 0797939; issued on February 28, 1979, in Pössneck; valid for ten years. On the inside, next to the passport photo, was the following information:

Name:	Strelzyk
First name:	Hans Peter
Birth date:	15 August 1942
Birth place:	Oppeln
Eyes:	Brown
Size:	Large
Marital status:	Married
Profession:	Electrician, aircraft mechanic

The Bavarian copied the information on the East German document onto a West German form. Then he asked the "questions of conscience" which must be answered by all East German citizens seeking political asylum in the Federal Republic of Germany.

"Herr Strelzyk, why did you leave the East?"

Peter answered, using the short speech he had prepared before leaving Pössneck, "We wanted to live as free people. . . . We were concerned about the future of our children. . . ."

In the Border Police Headquarters' building in Hof, at 10 Richard Wagner Street, Detective Heinrich read the protocol taken at the Red Cross station in Naila:

Balloon landing—Finkenflug (eight GDR refugees)

16 September 1979; 2:40 A.M.: Radio car 13–3 drove to Naila Army barracks. Telephoned report to Dobraberg radar station.

3:10 A.M.: Mrs. Künzel, Albin-Klöber Street, reported balloon landing somewhere in vicinity of Finkenflug.

3:20 A.M.: Car 13–3 approached by two men coming out of a barn. Abovementioned asked if they were in West Germany. Abovementioned very happy about affirmative answer. One man said that eight persons had landed in the balloon.

That day Detective Heinrich visited Günter Wetzel in the Naila hospital. And it was that day when the refugees discovered that, in some respects, West Germany was not so very different from East Germany.

First, two men from the Bavarian Border Police asked Günter for personal details—name, place of birth, residence, profession. Two other visitors stayed in the background until the Border Police left. They were heavyset men, about forty-five years old, with Bavarian accents. Both mumbled their names unclearly, both hesitated before they named the organization which had sent them. They had come all the way from Pullach near Munich to question the patient.

"We're from the Federal Information Service, Mr. Wetzel," said one of the friendly men. At first Günter thought that this meant some sort of press agency. But the visitors didn't ask the sort of questions that a journalist would normally ask.

Their first few words were warm and friendly: "We would like to congratulate you on your successful escape." But then the interrogation started: "Tell me, do you have friends or acquaintances there working for the State Security Service? Do you personally know anyone in the Ministry of the German Democratic Republic? Are any of your friends, acquaintances, or relatives presently in the National People's Army? Where, near Pössneck or in the rest of East Germany have you seen National People's Army barracks, Soviet barracks, or People's Police? Do you know where radar stations or similar facilities are located?"

Günter had no information to pass on to the men. And so they left, assuring him that these had been routine questions, asked all refugees, and that his answers would have no effect on his request for political asylum.

The next day Günter had another visitor. There was a soft knock on the door. The man who entered had rosy cheeks and greying hair. He was wearing a traditional Bavarian costume, obviously expensive, and a pink neckerchief fastened with a tie pin made of deer horn. He hesitated before nearing Günter's bed and seemed nervous, as though he were about to give a speech. Finally he came up to the foot of the bed and dramatically blurted out, "Don't you recognize me? I'm your father. . . ."

There was a good reason why, in fact, Günter did not recognize the man immediately. "After all," says Günter, "I was only six or seven years old the last time I saw him. And I never heard another word from him. He never even wrote to us."

It was not easy for Günter to carry on a conversation with the man. "How could I suddenly be nice to the man who had left my mother to struggle alone with no help?"

Wolfgang Wetzel, forty-five-year-old roofer, now lived in Kaufbeuren, a small town in Bavaria. He had heard about his son's escape on television and came to try to explain. In 1961 he had been sent to an East German work camp after an unsuccessful attempt to flee the zone. When he was released three years later, he tried again to escape. This time he was almost killed when he set off a trip-wire alarm on the border. The border patrol searched for him for days while he hid in muddy ditches in the woods only a few yards from the mine belt. When the soldiers finally gave up the search, he managed to cross the minefield and barbed wire to the other side.

"But why didn't we ever hear from you again?" his son asked.

Wolfgang Wetzel hummed and hawed, searching in vain for words of explanation. At this moment Petra appeared in the doorway and the conversation between father and son ended. Obviously embarrassed, Wolfgang stayed for a few minutes and left. Günter shook his head when he'd gone.

"Why did he leave us there alone? Why didn't we ever hear from him?"

This quiet reunion with his father only added to the confusion Günter felt during the first few days in his new home.

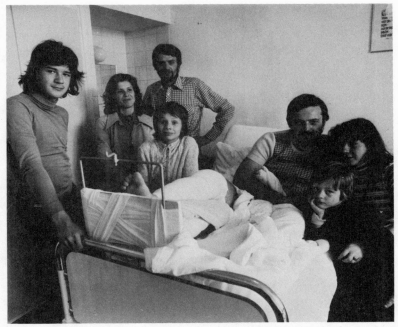

Günter Wetzel injured his leg during the rough landing and was laid up in hospital for several days. He is visited here by his family and the Strelzyks.

17

A
New
Home

Until the wind happened to bring the eight East German balloonists, Naila had been a typical little border town nestled behind the seven mountains of the Franconian Forest. The town chronicle humbly states: "In its one-thousand-year history, Naila had never been a point of interest." All that changed on Sunday, September 16, 1979, the morning that the German Press Agency sent out a rush announcement by telex:

gpa 057 pl/vm RUSH

eight persons in hot air balloon escape
naila (gpa)—daring flight manoeuvre from gdr
successful

eight refugees in bavaria: two married couples & four children
land approx. 1 mile west of naila . . .

A later announcement read:

gpa 076 pl/vm balloon two (naila)

refugees risk lives

glare of balloon seen 3 am by two policemen who thought house was afire. fugitives—37 yr old mechanic and 24 yr old

bricklayer w. wives & four children betw. ages 2 & 15—
abrupt landing, no fuel reserve—frightened. unsure they were
in west.

With suitable embellishments and additions, announcements
went out to all German newspapers and radio and television
stations, as well as to foreign news agencies. Naila became
famous overnight.

The young mayor, Robert Strobel, spoke to people from all
over the world: Canadian radio called, *The New York Times*
wanted information, the *Daily Mail* in London wanted an
interview with the escapees. Journalists from Paris, Rome,
Vienna, and Bonn arrived. Television reporters and photographers unpacked their equipment in the City Hall, filmed
the town, drove to the Red Cross station to film the refugees,
and hurried out to the Franconian Forest where the balloon
still hung in a few bent pines.

The little town of Naila and the eight balloonists from
Pössneck were suddenly the focus of worldwide attention.
Every newspaper in the Western world, from the tiniest
German provincial paper to *The New York Times*, seemed to
carry articles about the escape.

The *Frankenpost*, published in the neighbouring town of
Hof, wrote: "The balloon escape of the Thuringians is the
most audacious in years. Mere words cannot express the way
we feel toward the refugees. We can only admire them for
their amazing courage in the face of great danger."

The well-known *Süddeutsche Zeitung* commented in the
same vein: "The more we learn of the details, the more our
admiration grows. Eight people, two complete families, were
daring enough to flee East Germany in a homemade balloon,
landing with no serious injuries in West Germany."

All of the large mass newspapers in England appeared on
the stands the day after the flight with the same headline:
"Up, Up, and Away!" The *Daily Mail* subtitled its lead article "The most fantastic escape since the division of Germany:
freedom vs. death in a homemade balloon."

The New York Times linked the event to the forthcoming
thirtieth anniversary celebration, adding deeper political

meaning to the escape: "The dangerous flight of the two couples and their four children over a stretch of 28 miles on a small metal platform suspended from a homemade hot-air balloon says volumes. . . . The East German economy is suffering under the pressure of foreign debts and increasing prices of oil and raw material. Imports are limited, and the growth rate has decreased. A government which has pursued political stability by trying to please consumers for almost a decade is now being forced to tighten its belt. The balloon flight is a spectacular illustration of growing dissatisfaction among the population of the German Democratic Republic, contradicting the extensive propaganda for the thirtieth anniversary celebration."

In spite of all the chaos in his town, Mayor Strobel recognized the opportunity the event presented. He said, "No one had ever heard of Naila before and now they're printing maps in American newspapers with a circle around us!"

The mayor was a shrewd man and determined that Naila should remain on the map now that it was there. He did his best to guarantee that press coverage focused on the town, by helping the immigrants from Pössneck as much as possible. He offered them a choice of several town apartments, opened bank accounts for contributions, arranged for interviews, and hired a lawyer who would handle exclusive contracts for their story. He also made sure that the refugees, in particular the children, received underwear, socks, and shirts. And he was the first to tell the press about his good deeds. In private, he said, "Naturally, we are all very touched and excited that the refugees landed right here, and we will of course make the best of it for our town."

The mayor was convinced that Naila's recent fame would improve the town's image and encourage the tourist trade. The town had always been known for its clean air and streams, but it was too far off the beaten track and too close to the East German border for tourists to go out of their way to visit.

But perhaps the so-called death belt, only six miles away, could become an attraction and, together with the pure air and lovely hiking areas, would lure tourists and holiday makers to the area.

Naila, the refugees' new home, was at first glance not much different from Pössneck, the town from which they had come. A small town in Upper Franconia, Naila is situated in a hilly area, surrounded by woods and fields, 1,640 feet above sea level. It is primarily an agricultural town with some light industry. There are roads leading to the town from each direction. The church steeple in the marketplace, visible from far way, is the town's main landmark. As in Pössneck, there's a river, a main street, and a train station. The Culmnitz River eventually empties into the Saale; the local trains stop in Naila before continuing on to the Bad Steben spa, near Hof.

Naila's history can be traced back to 1343 when a colony settled on the banks of the Culmnitz and called the area Neulins. Copper was mined in the surrounding mountains from the Middle Ages until the beginning of the nineteenth century. Naila, too, suffered during the Thirty Years' War— not from the plague, but from a series of fires. It was granted a third-class town charter in 1880. Little damage was inflicted during World War II.

Naila boasts a machine factory, a leather plant, and a brewery. Most of its 9,400 inhabitants participate in men's glee clubs, small gardening clubs, sports clubs, or bowling clubs. There are several cafés here, and an ice-cream parlor.

Although Naila was similar to Pössneck on the surface, the refugees had only to look at the streets and shop windows to be reminded of the underlying differences. In Pössneck, facades were plastered with performance charts or Marxist slogans. In Naila, the propaganda was of another type. Here there were advertisements for Mercedes cars, laundry detergents, and various other consumer goods.

The day after landing in her new home, Petra walked into the Naila branch of the Edeka supermarket chain in the marketplace. "It was like an adventure into another world. There were shelves and shelves of noodles of every shape and size—long noodles, short noodles, wavy noodles, corkscrew noodles. There were even noodles shaped like little people! And they were all packed in cellophane so that you could see them. I had never seen so many colours of shampoo either—yellow, green, purple. It was amazing! The bever-

ages were in such pretty bottles that at home I would have
used them as flower vases. I thought that I was imagining
things when I came to the laundry detergents. They even
sold them in ten-pound packages!"

She had landed in the West less than thirty-two hours
previously and had already had her first glimpse of West
Germany's economic wonderland. It was too much for her
after only ten minutes. She was overwhelmed by the sight of
so many consumer goods. "I was dizzy and covered my eyes.
I didn't know where to look first, so I left the store."

The local stores in Pössneck had been markedly different
—colourless, lacking in product choice, and always plagued
by the chronic supply shortage. "Laundry detergent, for instance. I was lucky to find a small package every few weeks.
And whenever news got around that there had been a new
delivery, there was a stampede at the store. Here, the shop-
pers just walk by as if it were nothing special."

Peter was immediately aware of other differences between
the two ways of life. "It's so great to be able to say what you
really think, to read a newspaper criticizing the government,
to watch television and see people discussing politics. And
the people themselves seem more relaxed, more casual and
open, than back in East Germany."

Cars were parked bumper to bumper in the marketplace.
The people in the town were provincial but fashionably
dressed, and the shop windows displayed goods that East
German housewives could only dream about.

Masses of people followed the balloonists wherever they
went. "We went back to the balloon to make sure that we
hadn't left anything, and there was such a crowd that we
could hardly get through. Some of the people gave the children ten- or twenty-mark bills. I'm sure they meant well, and
in a way, we were touched, but it was a strange feeling. It
made us feel like beggars."

Mayor Strobel channelled the donations, more than 20,000
marks, from all over West Germany, into four different accounts at four different banks. Telegrams, postcards, and
letters continued to arrive in Naila from around the world,

even as far away as New Zealand, and were screened at the town hall before they were passed on to the recipients.

Letters were addressed to "the refugees of the year", "the balloon heroes", "the balloonists in Bavaria". A woman from Frankfurt am Main in the West sent the "courageous balloonists from East Germany" a pair of hand-knitted socks. An engineer sent a package with a suit of very fine English material. A doctor offered all eight participants of the "flight of the century" his warmest blessings. And Hermann Fredersdorf, former director of the German Tax Union, now head of the Citizens' Party, sent a telegram offering advice "in dealing with our state officials and red tape".

But there was reproach as well as praise for the East German refugees. Someone from Bad Homburg wrote, "You foolishly risked your children's lives. Your lives would have been no great loss, but your children. . . ." An anonymous letter came addressed to West German Counterespionage: "Careful! These are dangerous spies who have wormed their way into our country in a very sophisticated way."

Several enterprising companies tried to profit from the attention the celebrities were getting. A car salesman, knowing that the press would probably report it, offered to lend each family a car for three months. A furniture manufacturer offered chairs and beds under the same conditions. ("May we take a few photos when we present you with the furniture?") The Singer Sewing Machine Company, under the mistaken impression that Günter had sewn the balloon on a Singer machine, offered the families their newest model. When the newspapers wrote that Günter had used a Gritzner machine, Singer quietly rescinded the offer. An astrologist wanted to do charts for all eight immigrants so that they could prepare themselves for their new lives in the West. And so on . . .

There was no end to the attention. Even show business personalities and politicians managed to find ways to profit from the refugees' popularity. First on the scene was Hans Rosenthal, master of ceremonies for the somewhat inane adult show *Dali-Dali*, on West German television (most similar to America's *Truth or Consequences*). He invited the

Strelzyks, the Wetzels, and Mayor Strobel to Vienna for a live appearance on his quiz show. He greeted his East German guests with a smile, peered into the camera with an unusually serious expression on his face, and said, "What kind of country must it be that forces people to escape to freedom in this way . . . ?"

Franz Josef Strauss, President of Bavaria at the time, used this convenient opportunity to present himself to his constituency as a mild-mannered, fatherly figure. He invited the refugees to his official residence in Munich and presented each family the sum of 1,000 marks and eight silver coins embossed with his image. Press photographers took more than thirty pictures of the fatherly smile of the Chancellor candidate. "May I greet you as a fellow pilot?" joked Strauss, more to the journalists than to the refugees.

Strauss shocked Peter when he said, "In particular, I would like to thank you for your criticism of Herr Biermann who has taken a stand against me and proved to be a discredit to Germany." Strauss had obviously misread or misunderstood *Stern* magazine's article about Peter's views on the political critic Wolf Biermann. He thought that Peter had distanced himself from Biermann voluntarily rather than under pressure from the Socialist Unity Party. In fact, Peter had been forced, along with his former co-workers, to sign a statement saying that he disagreed with Biermann's opinions.

Franz J. Strauss had also heard that the refugees' families in East Germany were now being harassed by the State. He remarked, "They're just trying to frighten the people so that no one will try to duplicate your escape."

Indeed, the rumour had reached Naila from the East that two relatives of the escapees had been "apprehended by the People's Police". For several days it was unclear whether they had simply been picked up for questioning or arrested. As usual, the *Bild* newspaper mysteriously had inside information: "Entire family held responsible for political crimes of one member" read one headline. "Has the balloon refugee's grandpa been arrested?" ran the subtitle.

It was later discovered that Günter Wetzel's eighty-one-year-old grandfather had in fact been held for questioning but released.

Peter says, "I can imagine what happened over there after we escaped. They probably interrogated all of our friends, relatives, and colleagues. But I swear, no one knew anything about our plan. No one even suspected. We were careful to keep it a secret so that no one would suffer later."

It was months before the refugees could begin to live a normal life in their new home. They seemed to be a permanent sensation. Newspapers, television reporters, and movie companies continued to call them. Peter negotiated the rights to his escape story.

That wasn't all. When asked to dispel a rumour circulating in Naila, Peter answered, "At first we couldn't believe it either, but it's true. They're going to make a Hollywood movie of our story!" Walt Disney Productions, one of the best known and wealthiest of the studios in the American film metropolis, would bring the story of the two families and their giant balloon to the wide screen. "Of course, we had expected our balloon flight to draw attention in the West, but we hadn't expected a reaction on this scale."

What was their first impression of the West, a land they had previously only seen on television? Former Recognized Activist Peter Strelzyk says, "What I appreciate here the most is that you can say what you think. And you can go where you want." He is particularly impressed with the variety of political opinions in the West German newspapers. But, holding one of West Germany's tabloids in his hand, he adds, "Of course, there's a lot of intellectual garbage around too."

Petra and Doris were busy making homes for their families and decorating their apartments—the Strelzyks in a modern apartment block on the outskirts of Naila, the Wetzels in an older building overlooking the little marketplace. The two women had quickly got used to the well-stocked stores and Petra forgot her initial astonishment at the "mountains of detergent".

"Staples are a lot more expensive here than in East Germany, but on the other hand, there are things here that

The small town of Naila was thrust out of its thousand years of obscurity by the balloon's landing. Here the happy balloonists wave to well-wishers who thronged in thousands into the town to greet the new arrivals.

An entire group of West German factory workers laboured for a couple of days to repair the balloon. Here, the balloon is spread out in a quarry near Augsburg in preparation for a re-enactment of the flight.

Petra and Günter Wetzel go shopping in a West German super-market. Both families were amazed by the abundance of consumer goods readily available in Naila.

Robert Strobel, the entrepreneurial mayor of Naila, stands in his office. He became the official agent for the two refugee families. He hopes to put Naila permanently on the map through the fortuitous landing of the balloon in his town.

As an expression of their gratitude, the Strelzyks and the Wetzels presented the town of Naila with the balloon on September 21, 1979. The certificate pictured here commemorates the symbolic transaction.

would cost a fortune over there and are very reasonable here."

Günter, car fanatic and former owner of a Wartburg, wanted to buy his dream car—a Ford Capri. He no longer wanted to be a bricklayer. "I want to be a truck mechanic and already have a good job offer."

They knew better than to have exaggerated expectations of what life would be like in the "Golden West". Peter says, "We often worked sixteen-hour days in East Germany and we'll do it again if we have to." He planned to continue working as an electrician in the West. "As soon as I can manage it, I'll work for myself. My own little shop, that's my biggest goal."

Frank and Andreas attended the Naila School on Albin Klöber Street, almost in sight of the spot where they had landed in the balloon. Frank says, "We were at least one or two grades ahead in Pössneck. But I didn't mind. It made the transition a bit easier for me."

In time, the refugees could walk down the streets of Naila without being stared at. But they were aware of the fact that many people were envious. There were some who resented them because of the contributions they'd received, their apartments, and the money they were getting for their story. "People just assumed that we were accumulating a fortune," says Peter.

Naila's town council intends to honour the balloon flight as a historical event. They want to build a monument in Finken-flug on the spot where the balloon touched down. The plan is to build a seventy-five-foot wooden observation tower on the exact spot where the gondola bent the acacia tree before landing on the ground.

"Then visitors can come from far and wide to look over the Franconian Forest and the frontier to East Germany and see where the refugees came from," says Mayor Strobel.

The two families were offered more than 30,000 German marks by museums and private persons for their balloon, but they decided to donate it to the town of Naila. They typed a certificate making the present official:

CERTIFICATE
Presentation of a hot-air balloon to the town of Naila

In memory of our successful landing in
Naila on September 16, 1979, in a homemade
hot-air balloon, and in gratitude for the hearty
welcome extended by the citizens of Naila, we
present the town with our vehicle of escape.
This present is an expression of our heartfelt
thanks to those who have so generously supported us.

This balloon is a symbol of man's undying desire
for freedom.

Naila, September 21, 1979

The town plans to inflate the balloon annually on September 16, in honour of the day when the Strelzyks and Wetzels made their flight across the border to freedom. Ceremonious speeches will be held, and carousels, sausage stands, and tents will be set up.

Naila has already had a taste of things to come. In 1979, in a gesture of gratitude to the town and town council, Peter and Günter inflated the balloon on a field near Naila. A crowd of six to seven thousand people came from all over West Germany to watch the event. Traffic was so dense that Naila police couldn't control the jam of cars, and there were many rear-end collisions.

18

Repercussions

On the other side of the German border, police, officials, and journalists remained silent. There was no mention of the balloon flight anywhere in East Germany or in the entire Eastern Bloc. But in spite of official silence, news of the adventurous flight of the eight Thuringians had spread throughout East Germany by the following Sunday.

"As soon as they heard the first rumours, half the people of Pössneck sat in front of their television sets and switched on to West German channels," says the mayor of Pössneck.

Western correspondents stationed in East Germany reported that the spectacular flight was the main topic of conversation for days. It even overshadowed preparations for the thirtieth anniversary celebration of the founding of the East German Republic. "Even high officials talked about it at their official functions, expressing admiration for the courage of the two families."

In Pössneck the news travelled by word of mouth from house to house. There were small groups of people everywhere talking about the escape. In the factories the following Monday, soccer scores were forgotten and the balloon flight was the only subject.

Many East Germans felt a sense of triumph that the increasingly restrictive State apparatus had been beaten. Jokes began to circulate. There was the one about the People's Police, who usually work in pairs: Question: "Why are the Vopos patrolling with three men now instead of two?" Answer: "One of them has to keep his eyes on the sky."

Or another: "A little girl is standing in the Pössneck marketplace with a balloon. A man comes up to her, shakes his finger at her, and says, "Now, now, little girl, don't get any ideas about leaving us."

Traditional folk songs took on new meaning when sung by a group of young people drinking beer:

> Buy yourself a bright balloon,
> Hold it tightly in your hand
> And soon you'll be in fairytale land . . .

But here, too, there were negative reactions to the flight. Some said, "Sure, they risked their lives and they were inventive. But they're selfish egoists. We're the ones who will have to pay for their recklessness. The State will clamp down now. There will be more reprisals and more pressure on those of us who are still here."

For relatives and friends of the Wetzels and Strelzyks, this was indeed the case for the first few days following the escape. The publicity in the West probably accounted for the added pressure on those who knew the escapees.

About twelve hours after the balloon landed in Naila, several Moskwitsch and Wolga limousines with radio antennas were parked in front of the Wetzel and Strelzyk homes. The Stasi had learned the names of the refugees from West German television.

Both houses were searched from cellar to attic and several cartons, presumably containing evidence, were carried out. One particularly incriminating publication was the brochure comparing life in East and West Germany which Günter had carefully saved for ten years.

Several dozen people, all of them potential suspects, were questioned by the Stasi and Vopos in the first weeks after the flight. Most of them were released after several hours of questioning. Investigators searched everywhere for accomplices. But Peter was unconcerned. "No one, absolutely no one, knew anything about our plans to escape. They can't arrest anyone."

Peter was wrong, however. At 2 A.M., Friday, September 21, five days after the escape, two cars stopped in front of a duplex residential house on the outskirts of Pössneck. Four men got out of the cars, rang the doorbell, and went inside. When they left the house they had with them a man and woman—forty-five-year-old Horst Städter, driving instructor, and his thirty-nine-year-old wife Maria, Peter Strelzyk's brother-in-law and sister.

They were taken to an old building with barred windows on Torgang Street in Gera. This was the Ministry of Security. There they were locked in separate rooms and interrogated over and over again.

According to rumours circulating in Gera and Pössneck, the Städter couple had been accused of "aiding and abetting fugitives of the Republic". The evidence: Städter had sold his old Wartburg to Peter, and that was the car which the fugitives had driven to the scene of the launching. Secondly, an electric sewing machine had been found in the Städters' apartment. It was obvious to the authorities that the balloon had been put together on this machine.

Peter still insisted that no one knew anything about their plan, but his protests were probably of little use to his arrested relatives. He had been branded a "traitor to the Socialist Fatherland" by a unanimous vote of the Polymer Factory Party branch and banished from the Socialist Unity Party. Nothing he could say would have any influence over the authorities in East Germany.

More news came from East Germany. In the clearing in the woods between the towns of Heinersdorf and Oberlemnitz, where the two familes boarded their freedom balloon and took off for the West, some unknown East German citizens put up a street sign pointing toward the Federal Republic of Germany. The sign read: "Naila—28 minutes flying time."

Two days later, East German soldiers of the National People's Army discovered the sign and removed it, so that there would be no trace of the successful escape.

*The East German town of Pössneck, photographed after the success-
ful escape. Word of the flight quickly spread through the town and
became a heated topic of conversation, eclipsing even the German
Democratic Republic's thirtieth anniversary celebration in impor-
tance. Following the escape, repression was harsh, as East German
authorities rounded up several relatives of the departed families.*